THE LATIN PARTICLE
QUIDEM

JOSEPH B. SOLODOW

American Classical Studies
Number 4

The American Philological Association
1978

Copyright © 1978 The American Philological Association
All Rights Reserved

Manufactured in the United States of America by Johnson Publishing Compan
Boulder, Colorado 80302

G.

ELIGO CVI DICAM 'TV MIHI SOLA PLACES'

PREFACE

I am grateful to the Columbia University Council for Research in the Humanities, which through a grant helped me to prepare this monograph, and to the American Philological Association, which has undertaken to publish it. An anonymous reader for the Association and my cousin Dr. Elliott B. Urdang both made useful suggestions, and to them also I extend my thanks.

J. B. S.

New York City
June, 1977

CONTENTS

1. INTRODUCTION　1
2. OVERVIEW　13
   (Position of *quidem*, 16.)
3. EQUIDEM　19
4. QUIDEM
   I.A. CONTRASTING QUIDEM　30
   (Variety of adversatives, 31. Size of units, 33. Tendency to adhere to pronouns, 36. With non-parallel units, 43. Balance of units, 44. Examples, 47. *Equidem*, 53. Feeble contrast, or none, 55. Odd combinations, 56. Problematic passages, 58. Contrasting plus Adversative, 60. Contrasting plus Extending, 62.)
   I.B. CONTRASTING QUIDEM SOLUM　67
   (Similarity to Contrasting, 67. Examples, 70. *Equidem*, 74.)
   II. ADVERSATIVE QUIDEM　75
   (In general, 75. Examples, 78. *Equidem*, 81. Partial concession, 82. Adversative-Extending, 85. Adversative-Emphatic, 87. Adversative-Limiting, 92.)
   III. EMPHATIC QUIDEM　94
   (Definition, 94. Degree to which implied contrast is obvious, 96. *Quidem* displaced, 98. Examples, 100. *Equidem*, 104. Without implied contrast, 106.)
   IV. LIMITING QUIDEM　108
   V. EXTENDING QUIDEM　110
   (Range of examples, 110. Examples, 114.)
   VI. ALLEGED USE OF QUIDEM TO INTRODUCE EXAMPLES　120

5. QUIDEM WITH CONJUNCTIONS 127
      (Si, 127. Quoniam, 134. Quando, 135.
      Cum, 136. Ut, 138. Others, 140.)

INDEX OF PASSAGES 142

1. INTRODUCTION

The Latin particle *quidem*, though frequently encountered in texts, is complex and subtle and still obscurely understood. My aim is to clarify the use of *quidem* for readers of Latin.

To explain a complex word we regularly analyze its occurrences, breaking them down into categories. This is a sound and necessary method for capturing the sense of a language not our own, but it needs to be applied cautiously. The weaknesses in the explanations of *quidem* provided by previous philologists commonly derive from their analyses. The main difficulty is that the categories of *quidem* they establish have no center, nothing in common, nothing that persuades us that the word is a unit. The description of the several categories might as well be of so many different words. Ordinarily we ought to employ a kind of Ockham's razor and assume that one word or grammatical form has one basic meaning, from which the origin of others can be understood. This assumption is reasonable unless we know of syncretism or suspect it. It would be fruitless, for instance, to try to reduce the Latin ablative to one basic use, since we know it combines the functions of two or three earlier cases, the ablative, the instrumental, and, marginally, the locative. Similarly an account of the meanings of do, dare would be complicated by the knowledge that its proper root, corresponding to the Greek δίδωμι, has sometimes been confused with another, the *do found in abdo and condo and corresponding to the root of Greek τίθημι. But no such suspicion attaches to quidem, and we are rightly bewildered by the unrelated categories of its use that are postulated.

This unrelatedness becomes graphic at times, when different categories are dispersed throughout a work. Roby, for instance, deals with concessive quidem in paragraph 1621 and again in 2259 and 2261, quidem replying to an opponent's objection in 1623, restrictive quidem in 1692, cum quidem in 1732 and 1842, quandoquidem and siquidem in 1747.[1] Draeger scatters his explanation still more widely: paragraph 311.7 treats explanatory quidem, 311.3 quidem confirming and ironically contradicting, 332.2, 335.3, and 340 quidem in the first half of a contrast, 341 quidem meeting an objection, 488 restrictive quidem, 532 quoniam quidem, and 555d si quidem.[2] What consistent, coherent description of quidem can be gathered from so many separate comments?

Even works devoted wholly to quidem suffer from the

---

[1] Henry John Roby, A Grammar of the Latin Language from Plautus to Suetonius, vol. 2, rev. ed. (London and New York, 1889).

[2] Anton Draeger, Historische Syntax der lateinischen Sprache, 2nd ed., vol. 2 (Leipzig, 1881).

same defect. In 1880 Guilielmus Grossmann published <u>De Par-ticula</u> <u>Quidem</u>.[3] Despite the title, it covers the use of the word from the earliest writings down only so far as the age of Cicero; Cicero himself, because of his preservation in bulk and his predilection for <u>quidem</u>, naturally forms the heart of the study. Grossmann divides <u>quidem</u> into six uses which, if the word <u>quidem</u> were effaced from the text, could pass for six different words. The uses are Restrictive, Explanatory, Concessive, Continuative, Affirmative, and Adversative. Not feeling any greater obligation, Grossmann only hints at relations between these six uses of the same word. For instance, although on p. 6 he characterizes <u>quidem</u> as having a certain demonstrative force, on p. 22 he declares Restrictive the basic use; and on p. 44 he derives Explanatory from Restrictive <u>quidem</u> with an odd piece of logic: "quoniam notiones et sententias 'quidem' restringit ac terminat, haud mirum est, si Cicero aliique et prioris et posterioris aetatis scriptores 'quidem' particulae vim quandam explicativam subiciunt, quandoquidem explicare res complicatas vel involutas evolvere ac terminare significat."

As a result of not having any central conception of

---

[3]Grossmann's book was published at Königsberg (Regimonti). In the same year he had also published the dissertation on which the book was based. It is the book, identical with the dissertation for twenty-three pages and thereafter corrected and augmented, that is cited, and by the author's name alone.

quidem both Grossmann and most other students of the subject labor under another difficulty. They cannot allow transitional examples, in which two of the particle's uses can be felt at the same time; all examples must be pigeon-holed by them under A or B or C. How could it be otherwise? If the uses of *quidem* have little in common, it is difficult to admit that a particular example may lie *between* A and B. The regions of meaning identified in *quidem* are not contiguous, so there can no more be borderline points or areas between them than there can between France and Iraq. (See also pp. 65-66.)

The categories decided upon by previous students of *quidem* therefore lack flexibility as well as unity; they are too tight, too closed off from one another, too restrictive of movement. Though pedagogy requires some distinction of meanings, for we cannot embrace at once the full range of a word, even in our own language, yet a definition composed of such categories as described is false to our sense of a living language. The divisions between the uses of a word are almost never so sharp as dictionaries or monographs make them appear.[4] When we play with the different senses of a word, so that two are manifest at the same time, we are punning, though understandably no one ever punned with *quidem*;

---

[4] On the inherent problems of dictionaries, see the sensible remarks of Jules Marouzeau, *Traité de Stylistique Latine*, 4th ed. (Paris, 1962), p. 41.

but far more often--I might have said usually--a writer uses
words that reach out in several directions and cross the
boundaries of a dictionary's divisions. The word "mutabili-
ty" in Shakespeare's Cymbeline (II.v.26) has suggested to a
recent critic "philosophic, perhaps astrologically tinged
notions of universal inconstancy, of an anarchic variable in
the sum of human fortune" and also "the alleged infidelity
of women."[5] To be compelled to choose between these meanings is to risk missing the force of the passage. Examples
can be multiplied beyond count. The feature of language
that they point to tends to be neglected or subverted by
over-rigid categories of meaning.

Such neglect is particularly evidenced by writers on
quidem, who never once present an example as lying between
two well-defined uses. Yet examples of this sort abound, as
we shall see, and challenge the adamantine barriers erected
between the different senses of the word. Grossmann himself
reveals the weakness inherent in such compartmentalization:
without any sense of incongruity, without any mitigating explanation he often submits the same example twice, under
different and incompatible categories. He cites Cic.Fin.
2.118 on p. 26 as Restrictive quidem, on p. 62 as Conces-

---

[5] George Steiner, After Babel: Aspects of Language and
Translation (New York and London, 1975), pp. 4-5; in fact
he analyzes well the complex, interwoven meanings of the
whole speech.

sive;⁶ Plaut.As.2.2.5 (=271) is Restrictive on p. 27, Explanatory on p. 45; Cic.Phil.14.2 is found under Explanatory, p. 54, then under Continuative, p. 83; Ter.Eu.1.1.5 (=50) is termed Explanatory on p. 59 but Affirmative on p. 99; etc. Grossmann offers *prima facie* evidence for the weakness of his own system. Even if these were transitional instances of quidem, which they are not, he would have no way of dealing with them, so inflexible are his categories.

In part, however, Grossmann falls into this predicament because of a third weakness of method which he shares with others. Not only are the categories of quidem inadequately related both to a central notion and to one another, but they are also in themselves poorly defined. The most serious and most pervasive weakness in the explanations of Grossmann and others is that in defining categories of use they rely far too much on the *form* of the sentence containing quidem; they are mesmerized by the words surrounding quidem to the point of forgetting quidem itself. Grossmann's filing the same passage under two heads can in part be explained this way. Cic.Fin.2.118 (vos quidem) is counted an example of Restrictive because quidem follows a pronoun; but given the whole sentence (quod vos quidem adiunge-

---

⁶I have cited examples more or less as in the Oxford Latin Dictionary; occasionally I have expanded an abbreviation or cited from a newer edition. An editor's name without further reference indicates his comment on the passage in question.

re soletis, sed fieri non potest), we see that the _quidem_ is Concessive. Similarly Ter._Eu_.50 (si quidem hercle possis) is classified once as Explanatory, on account of the _si_, once as Affirmative, on account of the _hercle_. This is rank nonsense. Surely not every _quidem_ after a pronoun is Restrictive, and _hercle_ in no way affects the meaning of _si quidem_. Grossmann's work is riddled with this error. _Nam_ . . . _quidem_, _quidem_ with proper names, and _ac quidem_ are raised to the status of distinct uses of the particle, when in fact they are obvious combinations of common words, with their meaning no more than the sum of their parts.

Grossmann is not alone. The only other extensive study of _quidem_ suffers still more from this weakness, and indeed it does so in its fundamental organization. In 1891, eleven years after Grossmann, Antonius Ludewig published his treatise, _Quomodo Plinius Maior, Seneca Philosophus, Curtius Rufus, Quintilianus, Tacitus, Plinius Minor Particula Quidem Usi Sint_.[7] This work forms the natural complement to Grossmann's. (It is regrettable, by the way, that Livy, who after Cicero is the most extensively preserved writer of classical prose, falls between the two and is neglected.) Ludewig in details is more able and accurate, and his Latin is superior, but the organization of his study shows him even

---

[7] Ludewig's work was printed as _Prager Philologische Studien_, vol. 3; hereafter it will be referred to by the author's name.

more subject than Grossmann to the lure of purely formal categories. Ludewig divides all of quidem into three parts: quidem with single words, quidem at the beginning of clauses, quidem in one half of a contrast. The great and obvious difficulty is that this segregation of the examples is not at all useful. The categories are overlapping instead of distinct, so it is easy to find examples of quidem emphasizing a single word at the beginning of a clause, this constituting half of a contrast. Indeed, as we will see, such a use of quidem, which cuts across Ludewig's divisions, is the basic one. This is Concessive or, to use the name I prefer, Contrasting quidem, examples of which one finds in nearly every section and sub-section. In order to demonstrate this weakness of Ludewig's and to introduce the reader as soon as possible to this common use, let me quote the examples at length. Section I (with single words): A (strengthening, emphasizing) forma equorum qualis maxime elegi oporteat, pulcherrime quidem Vergilio vate absoluta est, sed et nos diximus in libro de iaculatione equestri condito, Plin.Nat. 8.162 (Ludewig, p. 4); B (explicating) no example. II (at beginning of clause): A (with one word at beginning) tempus quidem nullum est parum idoneum studio salutari; atqui multi inter illa non student propter quae studendum est, Sen.Ep. 72.3 (p. 25); B (with conjunctions): 1 (with et . . . quidem) et laeta quidem in praesens omnia, sed benignitati deum gratiam referendam, Tac.Ann.11.15 (p. 41); 2 (with et quidem) et quidem quibus adversus haec modis sit medendum verbosius tradunt . . . sed hae . . . in infinitum extrahendae, Quint.4.1.43 (p. 44); 3 (with ac/atque) ac primo quidem et sequente die tolerabilis labor visus, nondum tam vastis nudisque solitudinibus aditis . . . sed ut aperuere se campi alto obruti sabulo . . ., Curt.4.7.10 (p. 47); 4 (with nam) nam illa quidem priora aut testimoniorum aut etiam iudicatorum optinent locum, sed haec quoque aut vetustatis fide tuta sunt aut ab hominibus magnis praeceptorum loco ficta creduntur, Quint.12.4.2 (p. 48); 5 (with iam) iam quidem ex tota rerum natura damnosissimum ventri mare est tot modis, tot mensis, tot piscium saporibus quis pretia capientium periculo fiunt. sed quota haec portio est reputantibus purpuras, conchylia, margaritas! Plin.Nat.9.104 (p. 48); 6 (with preceding adversative) sed illi quidem officio functi sunt . . . mihi autem . . ., Tac.Ann.3.53 (p. 49); 7 (with si) si praestitisset quidem aliquid mihi, sed arma patriae meae inferret, Sen.Ben.7.19.9 (p. 53). III (in one half of a contrast): A (first half) all, of course; B (second half) no example. Though he does recognize Concessive (or Contrasting) quidem, Ludewig still is misled into considering et . . . quidem, et quidem, iam quidem, etc. as distinct and significant usages. Again, as with Grossmann, for whom the same demonstration can be made, categories are defined formally, with the result that the true usage of quidem eludes us.

So much for the two major works on _quidem_. I have, to
be sure, profited from them and availed myself of their col-
lections of examples. Three other discussions, however,
though too brief to be satisfying and too lacking in examples to be very useful, have lighted the way to my own explanation of _quidem_. B. Dombart, drawing all his material
from comedy, as long ago as 1869 offered a connected and in-
telligent survey of _quidem_'s uses, and his little essay,
among other good features, treated _quidem_ and _equidem_ iden-
tically, a position I will defend myself soon.[8] Though
briefer, Reisig's remarks are equally illuminating, since he
too tries to relate the different uses of _quidem_ to one central notion.[9] For him _quidem_ was basically contrasting, as
for Dombart affirmative. Both of these discussions are
hardly known or accessible, though they deserve to be.
Kühner-Stegmann finally offer a useful account of _quidem_,
richer in examples and embracing more idioms, but less acute
in its theory and, as in other matters, sticking too close
to Cicero (1.802-07, also 622). I have learned much, of
course, from editions with commentaries, although because of

---

[8] B. Dombart, "Beiträge zur Erklärung der plautinischen Captivi, mit besonderer Berücksichtigung der Ausgabe von Juli-
us Brix," _Blätter für das Bayerische Gymnasialschulwesen_ 5
(1869), 204-210.

[9] Christian Karl Reisig, _Vorlesungen über lateinische Sprach-
wissenschaft, Vol. 3: Lateinische Syntax_, rev. by Schmalz
and Landgraf (Berlin, 1888), pp. 272-74.

their format they are better suited to the explication of a
particular passage or idiom than to a comprehensive discussion of the particle. Many have been useful, but one stands
out above all: Seyffert's great work on the De Amicitia of
Cicero. To these works I am certainly indebted. As for
other treatments of quidem, all the dictionaries I have seen
are poor, Lewis-Short being the worst. Hofmann-Szantyr say
very little. Hand died after bringing his Tursellinus down
through the letter P,[10] and neither the Thesaurus Linguae
Latinae nor the Oxford Latin Dictionary has yet reached Q.

My own attempt to describe quidem is centripetal rather
than centrifugal: I have searched for the core of the word,
the essential notion which informs its uses. I have avoided
merely formal distinctions, except between Contrasting quidem and Contrasting quidem solum. I have tried to make my
categories helpful without making them unnecessarily numerous. I have included enough clear examples, I hope, to convince the reader and enough unusual or difficult ones to
alert him.

A synthetic study like this one has several limitations. Focusing on the word as a unit and drawing examples
from many texts, I deal only incidentally with the usages of
individual authors. This study is also unhistorical, mainly

---

[10] Ferdinand Hand, Tursellinus, Seu de Particulis Latinis
Commentarii, 4 vols. (Leipzig, 1829-45), referred to hereafter by author's name.

because the paucity and uneven distribution of the early material stand in the way of a historical account, but in part because I am looking for precisely the unchanging center of quidem; see pp. 94-95.

The subsequent discussion will be clearer if first I summarize my explanation of quidem.

2. OVERVIEW

Quidem essentially emphasizes, as has often been recognized, but it does so in a special way, always with reference to something else. Quidem emphasizes one statement (or phrase or word) while directing our attention to another which contrasts with the first, supplementing or modifying it. The truth of the statement made with quidem is always insisted on, however qualified; the other, contrasting statement is often explicit, but not rarely needs to be supplied mentally by the reader. The emphasis is created by the presence of quidem and by the contrast, which, varying in form and character, is translated by different words. An overview of the particle is given here, showing the connection of its various uses; greater details and finer distinctions will be found in the sections after.

I.A. Contrasting quidem. The basic use of quidem is to set up the first half of a contrast; some adversative particle is found in the second half. The contrast here arises from opposition and may be translated "to be sure," "on the one hand," or "indeed." This quidem is often called concessive. sunt quidem praeclara quae in publicum profers, sed non minora ea quae limine tenes, Plin.Pan.83.2. infecunda quidem, sed laeta et fortia surgunt, Verg.G.2.48.

I.B. Contrasting quidem solum. The adversative particle is often omitted without obscuring the contrast. Varroni quidem displicet consilium pueri, mihi non, Cic.Att.16.9. et tua quidem erga me munera, dum vita suppetet, aeterna erunt: quae a me habes, horti et faenus et villa, casibus obnoxia sunt, Tac.Ann.14.55.

II. Adversative quidem. Sometimes quidem appears not in the first but in the second member of the contrast. Traditionally this is called Adversative quidem, a name I will keep, but the close relationship between this and the preceding use should be observed. The statement "A, but B" differs from the statement "B, but A" in sequence, and therefore in emphasis, but not in the logical relationship of the parts: the truth of A is still insisted on, together with the supplementary truth of B. This opposition, made apparent only in the second statement, is expressed with "but" or "however." The halves of each of the following sentences may be interchanged with nothing more than a shift of emphasis. qui quid in dicendo posset numquam satis attendi, in clamando quidem video eum esse bene robustum atque exercitatum, Cic.Div.Caec.48. id nos fortasse non perfecimus, conati quidem saepissime sumus, Cic.Orat.210.

Other uses of quidem still show the particle's essentially contrasting nature, though more feebly.

III. Emphatic quidem. Quidem is often found emphasizing a word with which no direct contrast is made. We must supply the contrast, which may be definite or vague. For lack of a translation we can often italicize the emphasized word. (after talking about the two captives) hicquidem me numquam inridebit, Plaut.Capt.657, "*this* one will never laugh at me (though the other, who has got away, might)." istuc quidem . . . par omnibus periculum est, Liv.32.32.15, "*that* danger," where the speaker has in mind no particular other danger.

IV. Limiting quidem. A closely related form is Limiting quidem, which we usually translate "at least." In this case again the second half of the contrast is actually omitted, but we understand "A quidem" as "A (and perhaps no other)." ceteri Graeci Latinique auctores, quorum quidem ego legi annales, Liv.32.6.8. nihil sane ex me quidem audire potuisses, Cic.N.D.1.57.

V. Extending quidem. Referring back, like Adversative, to a previous statement with which it is contrasted, Extending quidem marks an advance beyond it, an extension or intensification of its truth. This quidem may often be translated "indeed" or "what is more." "scripsere" inquit "alii rem vorsibus"--et luculente quidem scripserunt, Cic.Brut.76. commentarios centum sexaginta mihi reliquit, opisthographos quidem et minutissime scriptos, Plin.Ep.3.5.17, as if to say "and they really amount to more than 160 volumes since they are written on both sides of the page and in a tiny hand;"

in fact Pliny's next sentence is: qua ratione multiplicatur hic numerus.

Other arrangements of the same material are possible. Limiting is so close to Emphatic quidem that it can be placed under it as merely a special case. Or the scheme can be altered to consist of three headings: I quidem anticipating a contrast (Contrasting, Contrasting quidem solum); II quidem looking backwards in its contrast (Adversative, Extending); III quidem with contrast unexpressed (Emphatic, Limiting).

Position of quidem. Quidem is post-positive; it follows the word it modifies and therefore is never found first in a sentence or clause. Sometimes it follows a group of words taken as a unit. re ipsa quidem, Nep.Phoc.3.3. post mortem quidem, Cic.Sen.74.[11] This can lead to difficulties. Thus, at Cic.Tusc.4.52 the MSS. are divided between isto modo quidem licet and isto modo licet quidem. No editor has accepted the latter. Wesenberg, followed by many, emended to isto quidem modo, in which quidem is attached to a demonstrative, as often. Dougan, however, prefers isto modo quidem, "isto modo being practically equivalent to a single word;" cf. nullo modo quidem, Cic.Att.7.22.2. Baehrens claimed that on occasion quidem precedes the word it modi-

---

[11] Jules Marouzeau, L'Ordre des mots dans la phrase latine, 3 (Paris, 1949), 100.

fies.[12] His examples are probably true, but his conclusion misleading. Alexander quidem urbem destitutam ab suis intrat, arcem vero, in quam confugerant, oppugnare adortus, Curt.3.1.6; the contrast intended is probably between urbem and arcem, in which case quidem is misplaced (Schönfeld: "Alexander drang zwar in die Stadt ein . . .; dem Angriff auf die Burg aber . . ."), but perhaps Alexander is contrasted with illi, "the inhabitants," the first word of the following sentence, in which case we have Contrasting quidem solum. et quidem cocum potentiae admonitum in culinam obsonium duxit, Trimalchio autem miti ad nos vultu respexit, Petr.47.13. Except for the obvious emendation of potentia to potentiae, this is the reading of the MS. All editors since Bücheler have read et cocum quidem to clarify the contrast with Trimalchio autem. Baehrens, however, argues that the MS. reading should stand. He brings in another passage to defend the MS. reading: ubi quidem parvo deversorio recepti, postero die amplioris fortunae domum quaerentes incidimus in turbam heredipetarum, Petr.124.2. He believes that quidem here modifies parvo--Müller now reads parvo quidem--but it is more likely to be a Contrasting quidem solum that opposes the two participial phrases, each dealing with one day's activity. Jacobs' proposal ubi ⟨tum⟩ quidem has the

---

[12] W. A. Baehrens, Beiträge zur lateinischen Syntax, Philologus, Supplementband 12, Heft 2 (1912), 393-94.

same end in view but is unnecessary. Apuleius has an instance: nam quidem feris et pecudibus os humile et deorsum ad pedes deiectum . . . nunquam ferme nisi mortuis aut ad morsum exasperatis conspicitur: hominis vero nihil prius tacentis, nihil saepius loquentis contemplere, **Apol**.7; **nam feris quidem** would have been expected. Similar is: nam quidem Diophanes Bithynius . . . et alii tamen obscuriores . . ., Colum.1.1.10. In all of these passages the **quidem** is not logically placed, a general phenomenon of which more instances will be found below, especially pp. 37 ff.

3. EQUIDEM

Before coming to _quidem_ itself, let us turn aside to the related particle _equidem_. Unlike _quidem_, which is enclitic, _equidem_ can stand, and often does stand, at the beginning of a sentence. It also differs from _quidem_ in that its use is more or less limited to sentences in which the verb is first person singular. Apart from this limitation the two words perform the same tasks. Once this has been established we may include examples of _equidem_ together with those of _quidem_.[13]

Equidem is clearly derived from _quidem_, but the source of the initial _e-_ is a matter of contention. The matter is of more than etymological importance, because, depending on our view of the etymology, we will interpret passages differently and even establish different texts. The matter is also of unusual difficulty, since our view of the etymology is formed on the basis of uncertain texts and interpretations. The rival theories are that the _e-_ is an intensive particle and that the _e-_ is an abbreviated form of _ego_.

---

[13] For useful, brief discussions of the problems with _equidem_ and for a guide to the earlier bibliography, see Hofmann-Szantyr, p. 174, and Duckworth ad Plaut._Epid_.16.

The first theory is that of Hand (2.424), Ludewig (p. 34), Kühner-Stegmann (1.805), Walde-Hofmann, Ernout-Meillet, and others. With ĕquidem they compare ĕnim, ecce, ĕdepol, ēcastor, in which the first syllable seems to have an intensifying effect. As for the varying length of the e-, it can be argued that the vowel was originally long but was shortened with the addition of an enclitic: thus beside ĕquidem we find quandŏquidem and sĭquidem (see pp. 36-37, below).

The rival etymology is less likely to be true, though accepted by most ancient and many modern writers. Festus (p. 462 L), Servius, Servius Danielis, Bentley, Leumann,[14] and many others as well derive equidem from ego and quidem. Whether true or not, this etymology at least reflects the fact that equidem is regularly used with the first person singular. There are two strong objections to this etymology. First, it is phonetically very difficult, even impossible, as some think. Second, there are a few reliable passages in which equidem in fact is not found with the first person singular; these exceptions seem to belie the proposed etymology. I suspect that the first etymology is correct, though both are operative in the history of the word. Equidem, I think, began as an intensive, non-enclitic form of quidem. Under the influence of a popular derivation from

---

[14]<u>Lateinische Laut- und Formenlehre</u> (Munich, 1963), p. 282.

ego it came in time to be restricted to sentences with first-person verbs; in comedy we still see signs of its earlier freedom. Linguistic purism sets in, however, and classical writers like Cicero, Caesar, and Livy invariably put _equidem_ with the first person. Then in later times we once again find a freer usage, perhaps because the artificial purity of the classical period no longer dominated writing and the two words became nearly synonymous.

Now for the evidence on _equidem_. Servius Danielis says (_G_.1.193): "'equidem' quod multi pro 'ego' accipiunt, id est 'ego quidem.'" And Servius himself states that for Vergil at least this etymology held (_A_.1.576): "'equidem' in omni Vergilio 'ego quidem' significat." Not everyone agreed, however, even in antiquity. Priscian's opinion is unequivocal (_Gram.Lat_.3.103): "sciendum tamen quod quidam 'equidem' coniunctionem compositam esse existimant ab 'ego' et 'quidem,' sed errant. simplex enim est. et hoc maxime ex ipsa quoque constructione orationis possumus intellegere. nam 'equidem facio, equidem facis, equidem facit' dicimus, et potest 'equidem' et ad primam et ad secundam et ad tertiam transferri personam, quod minime fieret, si esset compositum ex 'ego' et 'quidem.' nemo enim dicit 'ego quidem facis, ego quidem facit,' sed 'ego quidem facio,' tantummodo ad primam personam. et hoc usus etiam auctorum approbat, qui 'equidem' praepositiva 'ego' subiungunt, ut Sallustius in Catilinario: 'equidem ego sic existumo, patres conscripti, omnes cruciatus.' si esset enim composita 'equidem' ex 'ego' et 'quidem,' minime ei 'ego' subiungeretur."

Priscian essentially offers two arguments. One is that the phrase ego equidem would be redundant if equidem were composed of ego and quidem. To his example from Sallust (Cat.51.15) we may add Jug.10.6, 85.26, Rep.1.3.2, 2.6.2, and 2.10.4. (In Sallust's histories equidem is never found with the pronoun, in the letters invariably, in the monographs sporadically; see Vretska ad Rep.2.2.1.) From other authors we have: id equidem ego certo scio, Plaut.Bac.437; also Mer.264 and Ter.Hau.632 (where most of the inferior MSS. have quidem). sic ego, si iam mihi disputandum sit de nostris studiis, nolim equidem, Cic.de Orat.2.25. But languages can more calmly tolerate such redundancies than can the strict grammarian: witness in Latin such combinations as at vero, etiam quoque, ergo igitur, and even ille . . . ille quidem (as at Cic.Rep.2.21, quoted below on p. 39). This argument therefore is not persuasive.

Priscian's second argument is that in fact people do use equidem with the second or third person, as in equidem facit. He is on solid ground here, for, though he gives no examples, they can readily be supplied. Plautus and Terence in particular seem to offer numerous examples. Many of these are uncertain, however. The MSS. themselves often show confusion between quidem and equidem, as, for instance, at Plaut.Epid.497, Mil.650, Ps.620, St.329, Ter.Ad.555, etc.;

similarly et quidem and equidem are confused at Plaut.Per.
187. And even when the MSS. do agree, editors often emend
equidem to quidem, either guided by later, classical notions
of correct usage or influenced by the ever-changing theories
of Plautine prosody. Instances are Bac.974, Poen.1240, and
Trin.611. (For more examples of MS. confusions and editors'
emendations, consult the lexicon to Plautus by Gildersleeve
and to Terence by McGlynn.) Faced with this difficulty,
scholars at one extreme, like Jordan[15] and Hofmann-Szantyr,
p. 174, incline to considering false all equidem's with the
second or third person. Others, like Sonnenschein (ad
Plaut.Rud.1077), accept a great many as true. From the fact
that the best MS. authorities frequently preserve such equidem's and the fact that indisputable examples appear in later Latin, I conclude that such equidem's must have been used
in comedy, though in any given passage decision must be tentative. The following examples are all found in Lindsay's
Oxford edition: annos multos feilias meas celavistis clam
me atque equidem ingenuas leiberas summoque genere natas,
Plaut.Poen.1240. adulescentem equidem dicebant emisse,
Epid.603. quadringentos filios habet atque equidem omnis
lectos sine probro, Bac.974. quicum haec mulier loquitur?--
equidem tecum, Men.369.

---

[15] Henri Jordan, Kritische Beiträge zur Geschichte der lateinischen Sprache (Berlin, 1879), pp. 327-36.

Examples from later authors: scitis equidem, Sal.Cat.
58.4. haud equidem immerito Cumanae carmine vatis cautum,
Luc.8.824. non equidem hoc dubites, Pers.5.45. haud equidem mirum, Aetna 458. iam haec equidem ipsa vocis immutatio, Apul.Met.1.1. Apuleius' use of equidem is instructive:
all eighteen occurrences of the word in the Apologia and
Florida are with first-person verbs; more than half of the
ten occurrences in the Metamorphoses are not, however, and
in them equidem is equivalent to quidem (for some transitional cases, see below). From this disparity we may infer
that in the second century the classical distinction between
the two words was no longer observed in popular speech, but
only in formal oratory.[16] inlustres quondam quo praeceptore
fuerunt Constantinopolis, Roma, dehinc patria, non equidem
certans cum maiestate duarum, solo set potior nomine, quod
patria, Auson.Prof.1.5. cessabit equidem tortor et sector
dehinc, Prud.Peristeph.10.1101. More examples, not all
sure, are collected by Hand, 2.428-30, Kühner-Stegmann,
1.806-07, Jordan, and Burckhardt.[17]

It is indisputable then that equidem is occasionally
used with persons other than the first. Nevertheless some

---

[16] See Henricus Becker, Studia Apuleiana (Berlin, 1879), pp. 48-50; also Butler and Owen ad Apol.1.1.

[17] Jordan (above, p. 23, n. 15), passim; Georgine Burckhardt, Thes. Ling. Lat., s.v. "equidem," 5.2.720; to their examples add perhaps Stat.Ach.1.548.

of the instances offered only appear to violate the general
rule, but really show a transition from equidem with first
person singular to equidem generalized as an equivalent of
quidem; see Hofmann-Szantyr, p. 174. Sometimes the equidem
is placed at such a distance from the verb that its connection with the subject is obscured. atque equidem filium
tum, etiam si nolit, cogam ut cum illa una cubet, Ter.Ad.
850, where perhaps equidem is not yet far enough removed
from cogam to cause any confusion. In the following sentence some have mistakenly denied that equidem belongs to
scio: scio te esse equidem hominem militarem, Plaut.Epid.16
(the Palatine archetype had quidem--see Duckworth). equidem
credibile non est quantum scribam, Cic.Att.13.26.2 (two minor MSS. have et quidem); the equidem refers to the subject
of the grammatically subordinate clause. equidem si ex omnibus esset eligendum, nec diligentiorem nec officiosiorem
nec nostri studiosiorem facile delegissem Vestorio, Att.
13.45.3. Very similar is a disputed sentence in Livy:
equidem si nobis cum urbe simul conditae traditaeque per
manus religiones nullae essent, tamen tam evidens numen hac
tempestate rebus adfuit Romanis ut omnem neglegentiam divini
cultus exemptam hominibus putem, Liv.5.51.4. Weissenborn
connects equidem in sense with putem and explains that for
the sake of emphasis the clause giving the ground for the
speaker's belief has supplanted the statement of that belief
as the main clause. His view is right, and the Ciceronian

examples guarantee it.[18] Finally there are two odd passages of Apuleius in which *equidem*, appearing to modify an adjective, as elsewhere in his works (e.g. Met.10.1), may be influenced by a neighboring first-person singular verb. magnis equidem talentis, ut arbitror, Met.7.9. post multum equidem temporis . . . quievi, Met.9.2.

Another kind of transitional *equidem* is the one in which the particle accompanies not the implied word *ego*, but rather one of its oblique cases or its plural. This combination is quite common and suggests that *equidem* sometimes had a rather unfocused first-person feeling. equidem innumerabiles mihi videntur, Var.R.1.5.1; Hofmann-Szantyr, p. 174, remark that this is equivalent to *equidem innumerabiles puto*; we may compare: equidem mihi videor pro nostra necessitate non labore, non opera, non industria defuisse, Caes. orat.27.(Malcovati gives the text from Gel.13.3.5; Non. p. 561, however, reads *et quidem mihi videtur pro necessitate* instead. *Equidem* was probably confused with *et quidem*, as happens in MSS., and the rest of the sentence was adjusted accordingly, either by Nonius or by his source or by one of his copyists.) equidem mihi decretum est, Sal.Rep.2.2.1; Vretska glosses this as *equidem ego decrevi*. hic equidem

---

[18] W. Kroll, "Die Sprache des Sallust," Glotta 15 (1927), 304, is wrong then on both counts when he says that Weissenborn attempts to disguise the facts and that Livy is dependent here on Sallust.

Phoebo visus mihi pulchrior ipso, Prop.2.31.5. (The text is troubled, however. Two MSS. give eadem for equidem, which may be either a copying mistake or an attempt to "correct;" and the deteriores have Phoebus instead of Phoebo. I see no need to obelize the first phrase on the grounds of the unusual equidem. With Enk I prefer Phoebus.) me equidem certo servavit, Plaut.Epid.378, where many read quidem. per me equidem sint omnia protinus alba, Pers.1.110. iam pridem equidem nos vera vocabula rerum omisimus, Sal.Cat.52.11. quam olim equidem expotatus nobis advenis?, Apul.Met.2.13. istud equidem certe magnopere deprecanti concedas necesse est mihi, Met.8.10.

Though equidem instead of quidem is almost exclusively found with verbs in the first person singular, the reverse is not true. So we find both ego quidem and quidem alone with such forms of the verb. Cicero for one carefully distinguishes ego quidem from equidem, employing the former in his letters exclusively. This suggests that ego quidem belongs to everyday, colloquial Latin; in his more formal works Cicero wrote only the "correct" equidem.[19] ne hercule ego quidem reperio, Att.10.8.9. cui quidem ego semper amicus fui, Fam.11.5.2. Other writers are not so fussy. Plautus, for instance, writes equidem and ego quidem in successive sentences: scio equidem . . . atque ego quidem . . .,

[19] Georgine Burckhardt, Philologus 90, N.F. 44 (1935), 498-99.

As.842. But the phrase is wide-spread in Latin. egoquidem huiius servos sum, Plaut.Men.1071. atque ego quidem arbitror, Cato hist.95b. ego quidem vehementer animi pendeo, Cael.Fam.8.5.1. nam ego quidem vellem, Sal.Jug.24.9. ego quidem nulli vestrum deero, Liv.6.18.8. ego quidem percipio iam fructum, Sen.Ep.35.2. et ego quidem tres plagas Spartana nobilitate concoxi, Petr.105.5. ego quidem pro hospitis salute et homicida sum, Apul.Met.3.7.[20]

Neither equidem nor ego quidem, however, is required with first-person singular verbs. nolim quidem, Plaut.Mer. 539. vellem quidem, Ter.Ph.257. vellem quidem liceret, Cic.S.Rosc.138 (Siseby's equidem is not required). non sum quidem, Petr.127.6.

So much for the question of what forms of sentences allow the use of equidem. When equidem is used, it is used in all the same ways as quidem. That quidem and equidem are interchangeable is indicated by a pair of passages in which the same speaker uses nearly the same words, but once has quidem, once equidem. ego quae tu loquere flocci non facio, senex. meas quidem te invito et Venere et summo Iove de ara capillo iam deripiam, Plaut.Rud.783. minacias ego flocci non faciam tuas, equidem has te invito iam ambas rapiam, Rud.796.

[20]More examples in Burckhardt's article in Thes. Ling. Lat. (above, p. 24, n. 17).

Since *equidem* was understood as equivalent to *ego quidem*, it naturally tends to be Emphatic, "I for one," "I for my part." Suggesting modesty or at least an awareness that this is no more than the speaker's own view, it is often found with verbs of opinion like *puto*, *arbitror*, and *existimo*, often with "polite" perfect subjunctives. non equidem . . . existimo, Plaut.Mos.909. quantum equidem intellego, Cic.Fin.4.13. credo equidem, Curt.8.10.15. ut equidem arbitror, Plin.Nat.35.10. equidem haud abnuerim, Liv.5.33.4. equidem . . . non negaverim, Quint.11.2.23.

Examples of *equidem* are placed at the end of each of the main sections in what follows.

4. QUIDEM

I.A. Contrasting quidem

I have called Contrasting quidem the basic use. I mean that it most transparently embodies the essential nature of the particle. It cannot be proved to be historically the first nor is it at all times the most frequent use of the word. Examples of Contrasting quidem are to be found in Roman comedy, but not very often. A distinct and anticipated contrast such as quidem introduces sorts ill with the rapid give-and-take even of stylized colloquial Latin; or perhaps this use of the particle had not yet been fully developed or realized by the time of the earliest literature, which in general lacked a later age's more subtle and elaborate means of connecting sentences. But Contrasting quidem becomes frequent in the works of Cicero and, though found but little in his contemporaries Varro and Caesar, it continues to be frequent in the rest of classical Latin literature. Indeed Ovid, Pomponius Mela, Juvenal, Martial, and Apuleius use quidem almost exclusively in this way, Valerius Flaccus exclusively. Contrasting quidem is found on almost every page of Pliny's Panegyric and, used in such excess, it contributes not a little to the frigid feeling which pervades the speech. It is also especially common in Quintilian 10.1, where he gives a summary of the virtues and vices of many authors, for no particle is better suited to expressing the contrast of qualities.

Contrasting <u>quidem</u> very closely resembles Greek μέν in the first half of an antithesis; indeed, as we will see, <u>quidem</u> and μέν often work in similar ways. In a passage which he translates closely from the Greek, Quintilian confirms the equivalence of the two particles. non enim dixi quidem ⟨haec⟩, sed non ⟨scripsi, nec scripsi quidem sed non⟩ obii legationem, ⟨nec obii quidem legationem,⟩ sed non persuasi Thebanis, 9.3.55, "I did not speak without making a proposal, etc." The original is Demosthenes 18.179: οὐκ εἶπον μὲν ταῦτα, οὐκ ἔγραψα δέ, etc.

Since I do not want this common use of <u>quidem</u> to be mistaken, let me illustrate the variety that exists in the forms and natures of the contrast.

Variety of adversatives. Unlike μέν, Contrasting <u>quidem</u> is not regularly followed by any one adversative particle. We find the following:

<u>Sed</u>. By far the commonest of the adversatives after <u>quidem</u>. In Ludewig's collection of examples from the Silver Age <u>sed</u> outnumbers all its rivals taken together, 353 to 289; to judge by Grossmann's examples, Cicero uses <u>sed</u> ten times more often than any other word. de loco nunc quidem

iam abiit pestilentia, sed quamdiu fuit me non attigit, Cic. Fam.14.1.3.

Tamen. Common. illustri quidem viro, tamen plebeio, Liv.6.34.5.

Autem. Common. ceteros quidem ad spem proliceret arma sine noxa ponendi, ipsius autem ducis quoquo modo poteretur, Tac.Ann.3.73.

Verum. pulchra quidem, verum transtiberina domus, Mart.1.108.2.

Vero. et ceteros quidem omnis victores bellorum civilium iam antea aequitate et misericordia viceras: hodierno vero die te ipse vicisti, Cic.Mar.12.

Sed tamen. dissimilis quidem Chares horum et factis et moribus, sed tamen Athenis et honoratus et potens, Nep.Cha.3.4.

Verum tamen. dura quidem sentit esse, verum tamen usu putat posse molliri, Quint.8.3.32.

Ceterum. Common especially in Livy, Curtius Rufus, and Suetonius. laudavit quidem pietatem tanto opere pro se indignantium, ceterum et inlacrimavit et vicem suam conquestus est, Suet.Aug.66.2.

At. Lewis-Short, s.v. "at," II.A.a. η, remark that quidem followed by at is very rare. They are right. Among their hundreds of examples Grossmann cited none with at, Ludewig only six that are correct. The explanation for this rarity lies in the nature of at, for the description of which some other place will be more appropriate. et Themistocles quidem nihil dixerit, in quo ipse Areopagum adiuverit, at ille vere a se adiutum Themistoclem, Cic.Off.1.75. tu quidem ut es leto sopitus, sic eris aevi quod superest cunctis privatu' doloribus aequis. at nos horrifico cinefactum te prope busto insatiabiliter deflevimus, Lucr.3.904. Also Plaut.As.843, Ter.Ph.418, Cic.Har.30, Sen.Ep.71.30, 76.4, Tac.Ann.15.21, Quint.5.14.33, 7.1.39, 12.9.2, Suet.Aug.33.3 (MSS. have ad, ac, and a for at), Apul.Met.3.7, 3.22, 4.8, Fro.Aur.1.p.194 (79N), Aur.1.p.82 (3N).

Nihilominus. Very rare. magis quidem in iuvenibus apparet (sc. pudor) . . . nihilominus et veteranos et senes tangit, Sen.Ep.11.3; also Ep.29.4.

Nihilominus tamen. Very rare. aliae (sc. febres desinunt) sic, ut aliquantum quidem minuatur ex febre, nihilominus tamen quaedam reliquiae remaneant, Cels.3.3.3.

Atqui. Very rare. tempus quidem nullum est parum idoneum studio salutari; atqui multi inter illa non student propter quae studendum est, Sen.Ep.72.3; also Curt.6.10.5.

Contra. Very rare. et Romani quidem operibus magis quam armis urbem oppugnabant, Aetoli contra armis se tuebantur, Liv.36.23.1.

Size of units. The examples so far have tended to be short for the sake of economy and clarity. This is misleading. Quidem can be used to contrast units of widely varying size. Occasionally the contrast is of no more than one word. (Athena to Arachne) vive quidem, pende tamen, Ov.Met. 6.136. forte quidem sed indomitum, Quint.10.2.19. Indeed Cicero in one passage very elliptically omits the second half of the contrast: scito illa quidem sermone et Attico, sed tamen! N.D.1.93, "her style no doubt is the neatest of Attic, but all the same!" (Rackham). Far more often a double contrast is spread over two clauses. rex, inquit, semper quidem spiritus meus ex te pependit, sed nunc vere arbitror sacro et venerabili ore trahi tuo, Curt.3.6.10, where semper and nunc, pependit and trahi are opposed. Naturally the contrast often cannot be reduced to pairs of words: the whole thought of one sentence is contrasted with that of another. itaque bello quidem abstinuit; ut tamen expiarentur legatorum iniuriae regisque caedes, foedus inter Romam Laviniumque urbes renovatum est, Liv.1.14.3. nulla quidem sano gravior mentisque potenti poena est quam tanto displicuisse viro: sed solet interdum fieri placabile numen, Ov. Tr.2.139. This in fact will often be seen to be true, that quidem, though adhering to one word, really emphasizes an entire clause.

The contrasting units can be large. qua re quidem socium tibi eum velles adiungere nihil erat nisi ut in tua pecunia condisceret qui pecuniae fructus esset; tamen inductus consuetudine ac familiaritate Quinctius fecit, ut dixi, societatem earum rerum quae in Gallia comparabantur, Cic.

Quinct.12. In the following example a whole sentence intervenes between quidem and autem: Pomponius quidem, inquam, noster iocari videtur, et fortasse suo iure. ita enim se Athenis collocavit ut sit paene unus ex Atticis, ut id etiam cognomen videatur habiturus. ego autem tibi, Piso, assentior, usu hoc venire, ut acrius aliquanto et attentius de claris viris locorum admonitu cogitemus, Cic.Fin.5.4. multa quidem prohibent nocturno credere ponto. (There follow sixteen lines of examples.) sed, si magnarum poscunt discrimina rerum, haud dubitem praebere manus, Luc.5.540; Housman points out the correlation of quidem and sed. non quidem sibi ignarum posse argui, quod tam recenti dolore subierit oculos senatus: vix propinquorum adloquia tolerari, vix diem aspici a plerisque lugentium, neque illos imbecillitatis damnandos: se tamen fortiora solacia e complexu rei publicae petivisse, Tac.Ann.4.8; despite the intervening phrases, se tamen probably contrasts with non quidem, "he knew it might look bad to appear thus in the senate . . . but he hoped to receive greater consolation from carrying out his public duties" (see Koestermann); the se tamen may contrast not only with non quidem but also with the directly preceding illos. regressus in insulam rei publicae quidem curam usque adeo abiecit ut (44 words). ceterum secreti licentiam nanctus . . ., Suet.Tib.41.

Yet it is difficult for quidem frequently to introduce such very long periods as μέν does in Greek, because the anticipatory force is not so strong.[21] We cannot be certain whether a contrast will take place until it does. Sometimes, as noted in the Overview, quidem appears only in the second half of a contrast; and sometimes the contrasting thought is absent from the text. On this problem of identifying the use of quidem in a given passage, see below, pp. 65-66.

With pronouns. Many contrasts naturally consist of two pairs, and one of these is often a pair of persons, as in "he likes the city, but you like the country." Which pair is to be made prominent by quidem and sed, "he-you" or "city-country?" Latin has a very strong preference for contrasting the pronouns, and illī quidem placet urbs, sed tibi rus is far more likely than urbs quidem illī placet, sed rus tibi. In fact the attraction of quidem to pronouns is very marked in all uses, not only Contrasting; in Plautus we find quidem with pronouns especially often. A certain metrical phenomenon indicates the strength of this attraction. As an enclitic appendage quidem often shortens a preceding pronoun. Thus we find egŏquidem (Plaut.Epid.202) besides egō quidem, tŭquidem (Epid.99, Lucil.475) besides tū quidem, mĕquidem (Plaut.Am.749) besides mē quidem, and even hĭ(c)quidem (Capt.823--see Lindsay) and probably quĭquidem (Poen.

---

[21] Reisig (above, p. 10, n. 9), pp. 272-73.

1213).²² (By the same process sī and quandō are occasionally shortened when combined with quidem: sĭquidem at Mil. 520, quandŏquidem at Catul.64.218, Verg.A.10.105, etc.)²³

quid? vos, inquam, tacere non poteritis? nos quidem, inquit, facillime; sed tamen te arbitror malle ipsum tacere quam taciturnitatem nostram experiri, Cic.Brut.231. tu quidem macte virtute diligentiaque esto; ceterum qui auspicio adest, si quid falsi nuntiat, in semet ipsum religionem recipit, Liv.10.40.11. hos quidem vinxit, DC autem militum . . . interfici iussit, Curt.10.1.8. olim tu quidem adoptari merebare; sed nescissemus quantum tibi deberet imperium, si ante adoptatus esses, Plin.Pan.6.3. illos quidem senatus, me autem tuebitur Tiberiolus meus, Tac.Ann.6.5. nos quidem ad orbis terrarum extrema ut noxii pellimur et damnati, caritates vero nostrae Alamannis denuo servient, Am.Mar.20.4.10. With equidem. equidem attulisse rationes mihi videor, sed eas ita tu refellis, Cic.N.D.3.19.

So powerfully do quidem and pronouns attract one another that they often distort the logic of expression: quidem, displaced from the word it should follow, is put next

---

[22] See in general W. M. Lindsay, Early Latin Verse (Oxford, 1922), pp. 158, 73-74, and his edition of the Captivi (London, 1900), p. 25, giving earlier references. On egŏquidem see also Thes. Ling. Lat., 5.2.253; on tŭquidem Duckworth ad Epid.99.

[23] W. M. Lindsay, The Latin Language (Oxford, 1894), p. 216; see also Ernout-Meillet, s.v. "quidem," and (on si quidem) Sonnenschein ad Plaut.Rud.1061.

to the pronoun instead. This is extremely common. Ludewig, like others, has noticed this tendency of <u>quidem</u> to adhere to other words, especially pronouns (p. 3): "apud omnes post eam vocem ponitur, ad quam refertur, interdum tamen pronomini vel coniunctioni, non vocabulo, quod efferendum est, adiungitur." This is also true of <u>quidem</u>'s closest Greek equivalent, μέν. "Occasionally (sc. emphatic) μέν stresses a pronoun which seems to need no stress. (Similarly γε . . . tends to attach itself to pronouns.)"[24] The English word "only" offers similar examples of logical displacement that nevertheless does not obstruct the sense. By logical orthodoxy the adverb should modify the word before or after it, but in both speech and writing it is often harmlessly displaced. Consider "I only wanted to help." This "only" does not modify "I" (i.e. "no one else wanted to") or "wanted" (implying, e.g., "but I didn't actually help"); logic dictates either "I wanted only to help" or "to help only." Both of these alternatives are clear and unobjectionable, but so too is the given form of the sentence. Logical displacement of "only" is not more incomprehensible or more misleading than of <u>quidem</u>.

Cicero has a special fondness for <u>quidem</u> with <u>ille</u>, as is well known. (See, for instance, Seyffert ad Cic.<u>Amic</u>.20

---

[24] J. D. Denniston, <u>The Greek Particles</u>, 2nd ed. (Oxford, 1954), p. 360, referred to hereafter by author's name.

and 26.) verbis non ille quidem ornatis utebatur sed tamen non abiectis, Cic.Brut.227; logical emphasis would be **non ornatis** quidem. miraretur ille quidem utrumque, Phaedrum autem etiam amaret, Fin.1.16, for miraretur quidem or utrumque quidem. non illi quidem ut mihi stomachum facerent, quem ego funditus perdidi, sed certe ut facere se arbitrarentur, Fam.1.9.10; illi neither introduces a new subject nor makes a contrast. ceterae (sc. res) duce te gestae magnae illae quidem, sed tamen multo magnoque comitatu, Mar.11. hi autem ponunt illi quidem prima naturae, sed ea seiungunt a finibus et a summa bonorum, Fin.4.43; hi reveals how superfluous the pronoun is in this idiom, as Madvig points out. hoc, de quo loquimur, decorum totum illud quidem est cum virtute confusum, sed mente et cogitatione distinguitur, Off.1.95. nam princeps ille . . . aream sibi sumpsit, in qua civitatem extrueret arbitratu suo, praeclaram ille quidem fortasse, sed a vita hominum abhorrentem et a moribus, Rep.2.21; note the redundant ille . . . ille quidem. essent illi quidem desperandi, sed tamen essent ferendi, Catil. 2.10. dignus ille quidem omni regno, sed non per Fulviam, Att.14.12.1.

This idiom is not confined to Cicero. non ille quidem maior, sed multo illustrior atque etiam honoratior, Nep.Eum. 1.1. adfuit ille quidem, sed nec sollemnia verba nec laetos vultus nec felix attulit omen, Ov.Met.10.4 (adfuit quidem). velit ille quidem, sed dextera nondum par oneri clavaeque

capax, Val.Flac.1.110. summus ille quidem in his quoque
operibus fuerit, sed maioribus clarius elucebit, Quint.
12.1.26. gens Flavia, obscura illa quidem ac sine ullis
maiorum imaginibus, sed tamen rei publicae nequaquam paeni-
tenda, Suet.Ves.1.1 (see Mooney). et ille quidem . . . de
Alexandrina civitate mox fugit atque ad Palaestinam rediit.
ibi tamen cum cogitare coepisset . . ., S.H.A.Fir.Sat.9.2.[25]

Quidem is displaced to come beside other pronouns as
well. Displaced with demonstratives other than ille. est
ea quidem utilior, sed raro proficit, Cic.Tusc.4.60. his
quidem non omnino ingenium, sed oratorium ingenium defuit,
Brut.110. an esset hoc quidem proprium amicitiae, sed anti-
quior et pulchrior et magis a natura ipsa profecta alia
causa, Amic.26; Seyffert-Müller remark that sometimes an un-
emphatic pronoun is added to allow quidem to stand at the
head of the clause and that, as here, quidem often belongs
to another word or to the whole clause. est haec quidem
stultitia, sed ex parte quadam, non ex omni genere definita,
Inv.1.91, "this is a definition of foolishness, to be sure,
but only a partial one," though haec quidem might suggest
"this is a definition" (Emphatic quidem). Displaced with
personal pronouns. di me quidem omnes adiuvant, augent,
amant. sed quid ego cesso, dum datur mi occasio . . .?

[25]See further J. Samuelsson, "Der pleonastische Gebrauch von
 ille in Lateinischen," Eranos 8 (1908), 50-66.

Plaut.Men.551 (quidem is Bentley's emendation for equidem of the MSS.). atque egoquidem hercle ut verum tibi dicam, pater, ea res me male habet; at non eo quia tibi non cupiam quae velis, As.843. denuntiasti homo adulescens quid de summa re publica sentires, fortius tu quidem quam non nulli defuncti honoribus, sed apertius quam vel ambitionis vel aetatis tuae ratio postulabat, Cic.Planc.52, where the contrast is obviously between fortius and apertius. non tu quidem vir melior esses nec fortior nec temperantior nec iustior . . . sed paulo ad lenitatem propensior, Mur.64. ut his provinciis serius vos quidem quam decuit, sed aliquando tamen consulatis, Fam.15.1.4. bene plane magnus mihi quidem videtur, sed tamen non summus, Tusc.2.44. nam ego quidem vellem . . . sed . . . deprecor, Sal.Jug.24.9; ego is not part of the contrast. habes tu quidem fratrem . . . sed quid prohibet et sororem adoptare? Petr.127.2. tu quidem ut maximum recusasti; sed hoc persuadere nemini poteris, Plin. Pan.59.1. ipsas autem argumentorum velut sedes non me quidem omnis ostendisse confido, plurimas tamen, Quint.5.12.17.

The tendency of quidem to gravitate towards pronouns can present problems to an editor. Sometimes he must choose between the reading of the MSS. and his own sense of the idiomatic use of quidem. Thus, at Cic.Acad.1.18 all the MSS. have ut mihi videtur quidem, which Lambinus corrected to ut mihi quidem videtur. Reid concurs and points to a similar instance (Acad.1.40), where hoc quidem verbum is to be preferred to the hoc verbum quidem of the MSS.

It is especially common for equidem to contain a misplaced emphasis. The word was understood to be equal to ego quidem (see above, p. 20), but often it is not the ego but some other part of the first clause which is emphasized in the contrast. non equidem mihi te advocatum, pater, adduxi, sed viro, Plaut.Men.798, "not for me, but for my husband," where viro contrasts with mihi, not ego. equidem cupio et vix contineor; sed non minuam meum consilium, Ter.Hec.615. de quo dicam equidem paulo post, nunc autem hactenus, Cic. N.D.1.23. Lanuvio conor equidem in Tusculanum, sed faciam te statim certiorem, Att.13.26.2. vellem equidem vobis placere, Quirites; sed multo malo vos salvos esse, Liv.3.68.9. nupsi equidem peperique nefas, sed diligo talis, Stat.Theb. 7.514.

Occasionally quidem is displaced with words other than pronouns. et ceteros quidem omnis victores bellorum civilium iam ante aequitate et misericordia viceras, hodierno vero die te ipse vicisti, Cic.Marc.12 (either iam ante quidem or te vero). debes quidem adquiescere regulis, sed in derivativis sequere auctoritatem, Plin.Dub.Serm., fr. 95 Della Casa (=Pomp.Gram.Lat.5.144), (regulis quidem). vox quidem non, ut Cicero desiderat, paene tragoedorum, sed super omnes . . . tragoedos, Quint.12.5.5 (vox non quidem). vir quidem prudens et forensium negotiorum oppido gnarus, sed splendore liberalium doctrinarum minus quam nobilem decuerat institutus, Am.Mar.14.6.1 (*prudens quidem*). See also above, pp. 16-18.

With non-parallel units. Usually *quidem* and its adversatives are placed with equal, that is, grammatically parallel elements. Sometimes they are found with two elements that are not parallel, but rather subordinated one to the other. superbiebat ventosa et insolens natio, quod victorem quidem populum pasceret tamen, Plin.*Pan*.31.2; *quidem* goes with *victorem populum*, *tamen* with the verb; expressed more fully this would be "they were a victorious people, yet they had to be fed." ista quidem, inquam, Varro, iam diu exspectans non audeo tamen flagitare, Cic.*Acad*.1.3; *exspectans* is subordinate to *non audeo flagitare*, though the two parts are balanced by *quidem-tamen*, with *quidem*, as often, attracted to the pronoun: "I have long been awaiting them, but I don't dare insist." Similar is: iam enim ita clam quidem mussitantes, volgo tamen eum appellare, Liv.1.50.3. etsi facit hic quidem (i.e. ego, Cicero), inquam, Piso, ut vides, ea quae praecipis, tamen mihi grata hortatio tua est, Cic.*Fin*.5.6; the *etsi* clause, which cannot be a main clause, since such a use of *etsi* is found in the letters alone (see Hand, 2.600-09), must then be subordinate to the other; *quidem* and *etsi* are therefore doing the same job here; the *quidem*, though attracted to *hic*, clearly does not emphasize it. pulchri quidem et iucundi (sc. versus), quorum tamen hic exitus est, Tac.Dial.9.3; if the quorum clause is subordinate, this is another instance, but Latin, in which the introductory relative is common, cannot be pinned down so certainly here. cum Aequis post aliquanto pugnatum est, invito quidem consule quia loco iniquo subeundum erat ad hostes; sed milites . . . perpulere ut forte temere in adversos montes agmen erigeret, Liv.2.31.4, "the consul was unwilling, but his men forced him;" the quidem accompanies a subordinate thought in the first sentence, the contrast with which is formed by the whole second sentence; to take quidem as Adversative ("they fought, but the consul had not wanted to") is possible. haec lex socialis est, hoc ius nationum exterarum est, hanc habet arcem, minus aliquanto nunc quidem munitam quam antea, verum tamen si qua reliqua spes est quae sociorum animos consolari possit, ea tota in hac lege posita est, Cic.Div.Caec.18. Caesar Alexandrea se recepit, felix, ut sibi quidem videbatur; mea autem sententia, qui rei publicae sit infelix, felix esse nemo potest, Phil.2.64. ipse quidem certe cum sim sub cardine mundi . . . te tamen intueor, Ov.Pont.2.10.45. ille quidem incepto paulum ex sermone remittit, pauca tamen iungens, Stat.Ach.1.806. nullo quidem initio vel omnino vestigio cupidinis meae reperto, cuncta circumibam tamen, Apul.Met.2.2.

Balance of units. Denniston remarks. p. 370, that when, as often, μέν and δέ mark an antithesis of strong contrast, "the weight is far more frequently on the δέ clause." The same appears to be true in Latin, though it may be hazardous to cite examples. Instances of the two clauses being of equal weight are too common to need quoting here. In this passage the weight seems to be on the first clause: se quidem mori nullis supplicii causis, Rufrium autem Crispinum et Anicium Cerialem vita frui infensos principi, Tac.<u>Ann</u>.16.17; the speaker is more concerned with his own plight and mentions the others only to bring out the injustice being done to him; we might translate "I am dying for no reason, while they . . ." illi omnes quidem, sed Torquatus praeter ceteros furebat contumacia responsi tui, Cic.<u>Pis</u>.78. More often, however, it is the other way around: the <u>quidem</u> clause serves as a foil to the following one. So too we, when about to impugn someone's character, often begin "I am fond of so-and-so, but . . ." iis conloquiis aliud quidem actum nihil est, secutum tamen sua sponte est . . . ut vilior ob ea regi Hannibal et suspectior ad omnia fieret, Liv.35.14.4. urbes conplexus et alias quidem, sed notissimas Valentiam et Saguntum, Mela 2.92. semper quidem magnus, numquam tamen acrior quam ubi veritati commodas verba, Sen.<u>Ep</u>.24.21.

In the following examples the words themselves indicate the greater weight of the second part. rara quidem facie, sed rarior arte canendi, Ov.<u>Met</u>.14.338. vera quidem, veri sed graviora fide, <u>Tr</u>.4.1.66. Naturally many examples of non quidem followed by an adversative are weighted in the second half; the writer rejects one description or formulation and prefers another. sensi . . . quandam non quidem perturbationem, sed mutationem, Sen.<u>Ep</u>.57.6, "I felt a certain--I won't call it disturbance, but rather change." non tu quidem oderis . . . sed certe non probes, Cic.<u>Fin</u>.1.14. superiorem quidem numquam, sed parem vobis me speravi esse factum, <u>Fam</u>.3.7.5. cortice non scabro quidem, sed qui circumgelatus videri possit, Plin.<u>Nat</u>.13.120. deum, non quidem ordinarium, sed hunc inferioris notae, Sen.<u>Ep</u>.110.1. est alia non quidem reticentia, quae sit inperfecti sermonis, sed tamen praecisa velut ante legitimum finem oratio, Quint. 9.2.57. Atacinus Varro . . . non spernendus quidem, verum ad augendam facultatem dicendi parum locuples, 10.1.87.

Another recurring situation in which the second member is the more important is when the <u>quidem</u> clause summarizes, rounds off the preceding, and the following clause begins the next subject. The writer, as it were, plants his pole firmly in the river-bank and then uses it to push off in a new direction. This use of <u>quidem</u> is especially common in academic treatises, where the subjects to be discussed have been neatly categorized. It is noteworthy how often the first clause begins with <u>ac</u> or <u>atque</u>. ac personis quidem haec videntur esse adtributa: negotiis autem quae sunt adtributa . . ., Cic.<u>Inv</u>.1.36. ac de primo quidem officii fonte diximus. de tribus autem reliquis . . ., <u>Off</u>.1.19.

atque haec quidem et quaedam eiusdem modi argumenta cur sit divinatio ducuntur a fato. a natura autem alia quaedam ratio est, Div.1.128. ergo hoc quidem apparet, nos ad agendum esse natos. actionum autem genera plura . . ., Fin.5.58. atque haec quidem sanis facienda sunt . . . sequitur vero curatio februm, Cels.3.3.1. et haec quidem de dividendo in universum praecipi possunt. at quo modo inveniemus etiam illas occultiores quaestiones? Quint.7.1.39. et haec quidem auxilia extrinsecus adhibentur: in iis autem quae nobis ipsis paranda sunt, ut laboris, sic utilitatis etiam longe plurimum adfert stilus, 10.3.1. sed haec quidem inter se separata sunt. vis autem videre quem ad modum haec quattuor genera dicendi Vergilius ipse permisceat? Macr.Sat.5.1.13.

Examples of Contrasting quidem. hoc quidem actumst hau male. sed convenistin hominem? Plaut.Ps.1078. ea invenietur et pudica et libera, ingenua Atheniensis, neque quicquam stupri faciet profecto in hac quidem comoedia. mox hercle vero, post transactam fabulam, argentum si quis dederit, ut ego suspicor, ultro ibit nuptum, non manebit auspices, Cas. 83. non opus est dicto. --tibi quidem; at scito huic opust, Ter.Ph.1003. immo iste quidem rogat et supplicat: sed tu, quaeso, commovere, Rhet.Her.4.65. atque ego quidem arbitror Rodienses noluisse nos ita depugnare, uti pugnatum est, neque regem Persen vinci. sed non Rodienses modo id noluere, sed multos populos atque multas nationes idem noluisse arbi-

tror, Cato orat.164; not a very sharp contrast, "I think the
Rhodians did not want it; but I think they were not the only
ones." quae minus multa quidem alii, sed tantum numerum
culleorum scripsisse puto, ne cogeretur quotannis vendere
vinum, Var.R.1.22.4, "Other writers, to be sure, prescribe
much less, but he, I think, set the number of cullei so high
lest the farmer have to sell his wine every year."

civitatibus quidem suis non boni, sed certe docti atque
eloquentes, Cic.de Orat.3.139; quidem is displaced. utinam
quidem essent! verum tamen ut esse possent magno studio
mihi a pueritia est elaboratum, Div.Caec.40. iste quidem
tibi eripietur, sed nos non tenebimus iudicia diutius, Ver.
20. atque ille primo quidem negavit; post autem aliquanto,
toto iam indicio exposito atque edito, surrexit, Catil.3.11.
quae quidem (sc. acta Caesaris) ego nisi ita magna esse
fatear, ut ea vix cuiusquam mens aut cogitatio capere possit, amens sim; sed tamen sunt alia maiora, Marc.6; quidem,
though modifying the whole clause, follows the relative pronoun. nam illud Antipatri Cyrenaici est quidem paulo ob-
scenius, sed non absurda sententia est, Tusc.5.112 (Dougan
believes we must read est ⟨id⟩ quidem). non me quidem iis
esse viribus quibus aut miles bello Punico . . . fuerim . . .
sed tamen, ut vos videtis, non plane me enervavit, non af-
flixit senectus, Sen.32; quidem is displaced next to the
pronoun me. itaque mihi videntur omnes quidem illi errasse,
qui finem bonorum esse dixerunt honeste vivere, sed alius

alio magis, Fin.4.43. recte tu quidem, Scaevola, et vere: nec enim ab isto officio quod semper usurpavi, cum valerem, abduci incommodo meo debui, nec ullo casu arbitror hoc constanti homini posse contingere ut ulla intermissio fiat officii. tu autem, Fanni, quod mihi tantum tribui dicis quantum ego nec agnosco nec postulo, facis amice, Amic.8; Seyffert points out this contrast. Pollex quidem, ut dixerat ad Id. Sext., ita mihi Lanuvi prid. Id. praesto fuit, sed plane pollex, non index, Att.13.46.1.

novissimumque (sc. commentarium) imperfectum ab rebus gestis Alexandreae confeci usque ad exitum non quidem civilis dissensionis, cuius finem nullum videmus, sed vitae Caesaris, Hirt.Gal.8.pref.2. utinam quidem istud evenisset! sed eo non accidit, quod numquam cum fortiore sum congressus, Nep.Eum.11.5; Nipperdey-Witte give Cic.N.D.3.78 as a parallel. nam ego quidem vellem, et haec quae scribo et illa, quae antea in senatu questus sum, vana forent potius quam miseria mea fidem verbis faceret. sed quoniam eo natus sum, ut . . ., Sal.Jug.24.9. larga quidem semper, Drance, tibi copia fandi tum cum bella manus poscunt, patribusque vocatis primus ades. sed non replenda est curia verbis, quae tuto tibi magna volant, dum distinet hostem agger murorum nec inundant sanguine fossae, Verg.A.11.378. scripta quidem tua nos multum mirabimur: et te raptum et Romanam flebimus historiam. sed tu nullus eris, Verg.Cat.11.5. multa quidem dixi cur excusatus abirem; sed timui mea ne finxisse minora putarer, Hor.Ep.1.9.7. haec vox audita quidem cum omnium gemitu est, sed metum iniecit imperata recusandi, Liv.39.37.20; Weissenborn-Müller: "quidem gehört zu dem ganzen Begriffe: audita cum om. gem. est, besonders aber zu omn. gemitu, wie der Gegensatz zeigt." pauci quidem sunt sed vigentes animis corporibusque, 21.40.8. mors inhonesta quidem, tu moriere tamen, Prop.2.8.28. ille quidem ferus est et qui mihi saepe repugnet; sed puer est, aetas mollis et apta regi, Ov.A.A.1.9. vellet abesse quidem, sed adest, Met.3.247. o mihi care quidem semper, sed tempore duro cognite, Tr.3.4.1.

quae vera quidem sunt; a communibus tamen ad quaedam propria descendunt, nisi persuadere nobis volunt sanis quidem considerandum esse, quod caelum, quod tempus anni sit, aegris vero non esse, Cels.proem.71, a double example. similes quidem sed tamen dispares poenas, Curt.5.5.7. vaste quidem in latitudinem patens, qua penetrat tamen vastius, Mela 2.55. et ille quidem animam ebulliit, et ex eo desiit vivere videri. exspiravit autem dum comoedos audit, Sen. Apoc.4.2. quemadmodum radii solis contingunt quidem terram sed ibi sunt unde mittuntur, sic animus magnus ac sacer et in hoc demissus, ut propius divina nossemus, conversatur quidem nobiscum sed haeret origini suae, Ep.41.5. multarum quidem rerum oblivionem sentiunt, sed multarum et imitantur, Dial.10.12.8. omnia quidem deorum esse, sed non omnia dis dedicata, Ben.7.7.3.

vites . . . numero quidem perpaucas, verum ita fertiles ut in iugo singulae ternas urnas praeberent, Colum.3.9.2. Numa Romulo successerit ex Sabinis veniens, vicinus quidem, sed tunc externus, Inscr. Dessau 212. populi, iam quidem infecti, nondum tamen Aethiopum modo exusti, Plin.Nat.6.70. oratores quidem ambo, sed tam dispari eventu, Nat.7.165. fama quidem generi Phasias me duxit ad urbes, sed tamen et vestri, Luc.10.184. Ascyltos quidem paulisper obstupuit, ego autem frigidior hieme Gallica factus nullum potui verbum emittere, Petr.19.3. ac veterum quidem sapientiae professorum multos et honesta praecepisse et, ut praeceperint, etiam vixisse facile concesserim: nostris vero temporibus sub hoc nomine maxima in plerisque vitia latuerunt, Quint. 1.pref.15. Cicero quidem initium orandi conditoribus urbium ac legum latoribus dedit, in quibus fuisse vim dicendi necesse est: cur tamen hanc primam originem putet non video, 3.2.4. lascivus quidem in herois quoque Ovidius et nimium amator ingenii sui, laudandus tamen partibus, 10.1.88.

marmora parva quidem sed non cessura, viator, Mausoli saxis pyramidumque legis, Mart.10.63.1. magna quidem, sacris quae dat praecepta libellis, victrix fortunae sapientia; ducimus autem hos quoque felices, qui ferre incommoda vitae nec iactare iugum vita didicere magistra, Juv.13.19. ille quidem ramis insontis olivae pacificus, sed bella ciet, Stat.Theb.12.682. saeva quidem lucis miseris mora; dent tamen oro unum illum mihi fata diem, Val.Flac.6.733. disertam quidem, sed inexercitatam et eius modi certaminum rudem Helvidii sapientiam, Tac.Dial.5.7. non quidem in bello sed pro pace, Hist.1.63. non quidem sibi ignara quae de Silano vulgabantur, sed non ex rumore statuendum, Ann.3.69; non quidem . . . sed is common in Tacitus, being found also at Dial.3.2, Ann.4.7, 5.5, 6.50, 15.71. et Aurelia quidem vivit, ille tamen istud tamquam morituram coegit, Plin.Ep. 2.20.11. Corinthium signum, modicum quidem sed festivum et expressum, Ep.3.6.1. obsequens Nilus Aegypto quidem saepe, sed gloriae nostrae numquam largior fluxit, Pan.31.6. tibi quidem secundum exempla complurium in mentem venit posse collegium fabrorum apud Nicomedenses constitui. sed meminerimus provinciam istam et praecipue eas civitates eius modi factionibus esse vexatas, Traj. in Plin.Ep.10.34.1. hanc quidem actionem deposuit. ceterum Caecilio Metello . . . auctorem propugnatoremque se pertinacissime praestitit, Suet.Jul.15.

et Zamam quidem frustra adsiluit; ceterum Thalam gravem armis thensaurisque regis diripuit, Flor.Epit.1.36 (3.1.11). voluntatem quidem tuam magno opere probavi laudavique, quom verbum quaerere adgressus es; indiligentiam autem quaesiti verbi, quod esset absurdum, reprehendi, Fro.Aur.1.p.10 (61N). Graecum quidem mire quam suave est, verti autem neque debuit neque potuit, Gel.9.9.4; Contrasting quidem is very common in Gellius. sed mihi sero quidem, serio tamen subvenit ad auxilium civile decurrere, Apul.Met.3.29. fani quidem advena, religionis autem indigena, Met.11.26. per se 'super' significat quidem 'supra' . . . verum ponitur etiam pro 'de,' Fest. p.394 L, "means 'above' but is also used for 'about.'" argutias quidem laudare, ea vero quae recta sunt eligere probare suscipere, Min.Fel.Oct.14.7.

haec ita illecebrosius atque inhumanius agi loquebatur quidem pertinax rumor, Valentinianus vero tamquam auribus cera illitis ignorabat, Am.Mar.30.5.7. virum bonum quidem sed longe a moribus Probi, S.H.A.Prob.24.4. et erant quidem discordiae inter Balbinum et Maximum, sed tacitae et quae intellegerentur potius quam viderentur, Max.Balb.14.1. illa quidem flatus Domini est, sed spiritus et vis non est plena Dei, Prud.Apoth.830. ut crateres quidem implacabiles, Palici autem placabiles vocarentur, Macr.Sat.5.19.21. erunt quidem magni leones, sed minime armentis nocebunt, Serv.Ecl. 4.22.

Examples of Contrasting equidem. meruisse equidem me maxumum fateor malum et tuae fecisse me hospitae aio iniuriam; sed meam esse erilem concubinam censui, Plaut.Mil.547. occidam illum equidem et vincam, si id quaeritis, inquit. verum illud credo fore: in os prius accipiam ipse, quam gladium in stomacho furia ac pulmonibu' sisto, Lucil.153. occidar equidem, sed victus non peribo, Rhet.Her.4.65 (some MSS. have occidere equidem). audivi equidem ista, inquam, de maioribus natu, sed numquam sum adductus ut crederem,

Cic.Brut.100. equidem dolui; ὁ δ' οὐκ ἐμπάζετο μύθων, Att.
4.7.3. quos equidem facillime sustineo, sed impediunt tamen, Fam.11.14.2. equidem . . . putabam . . . ceterum
. . ., Sal.Hist.1.77.6; Jacobs-Wirz-Kurfess point out the
contrast between the equidem and ceterum clauses. non equidem extimui Danaum quod ductor et Arcas quodque a stirpe
fores geminis coniunctus Atridis; sed mea me virtus et
sancta oracula divum . . . coniunxere tibi, Verg.A.8.129.
non equidem insector delendave carmina Livi esse reor . . .
sed emendata videri pulchraque et exactis minimum distantia
miror, Hor.Ep.2.1.69. The following example demonstrates
how close quidem/equidem is to Greek μέν : neminem equidem
timeo praeter deos immortalis; non omnium autem credo fidei
quos circa te video, atque omnium minime Aetolis, Liv.32.32.
14, a translation of Polyb.18.1.7: φοβεῖσθαι μὲν ἔφησεν
ὁ Φίλιππος οὐδένα πλὴν τοὺς θεούς, ἀπιστεῖν δὲ τοῖς πλείστοις
τῶν παρόντων, μάλιστα δ' Αἰτωλοῖς.

non equidem invideo: numquid tamen ulla feritur quae
sterilis sola conspicienda coma est? Nux 33. vix equidem
memini, memini tamen, Ov.Ep.8.75. equidem cuius criminis
reus sim non video. . . . atqui coniurationis caput me fuisse credit rex! Curt.6.10.5. equidem primam omnium illam
cogitationem hominum . . . deprecor, ne quasi novam istam
rem introduci exhorrescatis, sed illa potius cogitetis, quam
multa in hac civitate novata sint, Inscr. Dessau 212. invehi peregrinas merces conciliarique externa pretia displic-

uisse maioribus crediderim equidem, non tamen hoc Catonem providisse, cum damnaret artem, Plin.Nat.29.24. quem non equidem omnino conabar excutere, sed potioribus praeferri non sinebam, Quint.10.1.126. vereor, fidissime coniunx, nil equidem; miserere tamen promissaque serva, Val.Flac.8.420. defleo equidem filium meum semperque deflebo; sed neque reum prohibeo quo minus cuncta proferat, quibus innocentia eius sublevari aut . . . coargui possit, Tac.Ann.3.12.

Feeble contrast. In the foregoing examples the contrast or opposition, though perhaps otiose on occasion, was clear and real. Sometimes the contrast can be weak or even perfunctory; the writer employs words that indicate a contrast, but the substance of it does not exist. formam quidem ipsam, Marce fili, et tamquam faciem honesti vides, quae si oculis cerneretur, mirabiles amores, ut ait Plato, excitaret sapientiae. sed omne quod est honestum id quattuor partium oritur ex aliqua, Cic.Off.1.15.

No contrast. Occasionally in Latin, and very much more rarely than with Greek μέν and δέ , the units linked by quidem and its adversative are antithetical without opposition or contrast at all; they are allies, not enemies. vita quidem talis fuit vel fortuna vel gloria ut nihil posset accedere, moriendi autem sensum celeritas abstulit, Cic.Amic. 12. The words vita and moriendi are opposites, and this may have suggested the antithesis. But the thoughts are not opposed to one another in any way; instead they are complementary and point out two sides of Scipio's good fortune. Even clearer is this passage: Athenas inde, plenas quidem et ipsas vetustae famae, multa tamen visenda habentis, Liv. 45.27.11; again the two parts are complementary, for Athens' ancient fame and its attractions for tourists do not contrast with one another; Weissenborn-Müller, in order to evince an antithesis, strain the Latin somewhat when they say, "Athen bot zwar gleichfalls vieles, was nur wegen des hohen Alters gefeiert war, aber auch vieles Grossartige, das seiner selbst wegen und noch damals sehenswert war."

Odd combinations. The extent to which the contrasting value of quidem with an adversative can be enfeebled may be seen from some odd expressions found mainly in Pliny the Elder and collected by Ludewig, pp. 45-46; see also Grossmann, pp. 69-70. It is obvious, on the one hand, that expressions like quidem . . . sed et (etiam, maxime, etc.) are not distinct enough to warrant a new category; they merely constitute a particular form of Contrasting quidem in which the second half opposes and corrects the narrowness of the first. nam omnia male facta vostra repperi radicitus, non radicitus quidem verum etiam exradicitus, Plaut.Mos.1112; the quidem may at the same time be Adversative, correcting the previous radicitus, as Fay suggests (see also below, pp. 60-62). in Hispaniam ad te maxime ille quidem suo consilio, sed etiam me auctore est profectus, Cic.Fam.13.16.3.

haematitis in Aethiopia quidem principalis est, sed et in Arabia et in Africa invenitur, Plin.Nat.37.169. est ergo, ut dicebam, clementia omnibus quidem hominibus secundum naturam, maxime tamen decora imperatoribus, Sen.Cl.1.5.2. quo vitio multi quidem laborarunt, praecipue tamen Hermagoras, Quint.3.11.22.

When, on the other hand, we find non quidem solum . . . sed etiam, et quidem . . . et, et quidem . . . sed et, and et quidem . . . sed praecipue, we must recognize that the contrasting force of quidem has been so diminished that the particle can be combined with expressions not strictly compatible. Cicero goes only slightly beyond the examples of the previous paragraph when he says: non centurioni quidem solum, sed equiti etiam Romano, Phil.1.20. But even this phrase, a marriage of non solum . . . sed etiam with quidem . . . sed which is not repeated anywhere in Latin, is slightly mismatched; for the first partner demands equality in its domain, the second contrast. The other idioms are located only in Pliny the Elder and show the same weakening of quidem. et alia quidem fabulosa et urbes multas ab eo conditas, Nat.5.8. This unique et quidem . . . et resembles the Ciceronian misalliance. The other instance of et quidem . . . et alleged by Ludewig is: namque et nunc quidem solvuntur et tum erant notiora, cum dicerentur: aenigmata sunt tamen, Quint.8.6.53. The quidem, however, does not go with nunc solvuntur alone; rather it contrasts the whole first

clause, namque . . . dicerentur, with the second, aenigmata
sunt tamen; compare the very similar sentence at 5.10.43.
This Plautine passage may be a parallel, however: et quidem
servos et liber fuisti, et ego me confido fore, Capt.574.
The second idiom is et quidem . . . sed et. et alienus quidem sed et suus, Plin.Nat.15.107. caryotae . . . et cibo
quidem sed et suco uberrimae, 13.44. et hic quidem, sed et
mullus ac laser, 32.25; also 18.101 and 19.74. This, like
the first Plinian idiom, is a monstrosity, a fabulous and
illogical hybrid like a centaur. It is uncertain whether we
should take it as et quidem . . . et with an added sed or as
a combination of quidem . . . sed and et . . . et. In
either case we note the much diminished force of quidem, as
also in the following passages. Indi et alias quidem gemmas
. . . adulterare invenerunt, sed praecipue berullos, 37.79.
ab exitio et iumentorum quidem, sed praecipue caprarum,
21.74; also 22.36 and 32.25.

Problematic passages. Contrasting quidem may be con-
cealed to the reader's eye by the size of the elements contrasted, by their lack of parallelism, by the displacement
of quidem, and by the varying quality of its contrast.
These, however, are superficial obstacles, and I hope to
have overcome them. Still, other problems remain, and these
will lead us into some more general matters having to do
with our particle.

In each of the following passages <u>quidem</u> is followed by two adversatives either of which may look back to <u>quidem</u>. On reflection one or the other appears to mark the intended antithesis; but how does the reader as he works through the passage know this? ⟨qui⟩ quidem semper erunt clari, conscientia vero facti sui etiam beati; sed nos, nisi me fallit, iacebimus, Cic.<u>Att</u>.14.12.2; <u>qui</u> is contrasted with <u>nos</u>. Metrodorus quidem perfecte eum beatum putat, cui corpus bene constitutum sit et exploratum ita semper fore. quis autem est iste, cui id exploratum possit esse? Epicurus vero ea dicit, ut mihi quidem risus captare videatur, <u>Tusc</u>.2.17, the <u>quidem</u> after <u>mihi</u> being Emphatic or Limiting. haec metuo equidem ne sint somnia, sed tamen M'. Lepidum, L. Torquatum, C. Cassium . . . Philotimi litterae ad vitam revocaverunt. ego autem illa metuo ne veriora sint, nos omnis paene iam captos esse, <u>Att</u>.7.23.1; the emphasized part of the first half is <u>haec</u>, not <u>ego</u>, and it is contrasted with <u>illa</u> in the following sentence, not with <u>sed</u> <u>tamen</u>. bonus quidem et dicet saepius vera atque honesta. sed etiam si quando . . . falso haec adfirmare conabitur, maiore cum fide necesse est audiatur. at malis hominibus ex contemptu opinionis et ignorantia recti nonnumquam excidit ipsa simulatio, Quint. 12.1.11. In the next example <u>quidem</u> may be Contrasting (with <u>ad</u> <u>Parthicum</u> <u>vero</u> <u>bellum</u>) or Contrasting <u>quidem</u> <u>solum</u> (with <u>contra</u> <u>Chattos</u>): et adversus Britannos quidem Calpurnius Agricola missus est, contra Chattos Aufidius Victorinus. ad Parthicum vero bellum senatu consentiente Verus frater est missus, S.H.A.M.Ant.8.8.

The problem with this next passage is that the author switches horses in the middle of the stream. quare artes quidem et consilia lateant et quidquid si deprenditur perit. hactenus eloquentia secretum habet. verborum quidem dilectus, gravitas sententiarum, figurarum elegantia aut non sunt aut apparent: sed vel propter hoc ipsum ostentanda non sunt, quod apparent, Quint.12.9.5-6. Quintilian at first intended to contrast artes and consilia, which must be hidden, with other rhetorical adornments, which must be manifest. The first quidem then is Contrasting. After the intervention of a short sentence, however, Quintilian, either forgetting what he had written or catching sight of a new contrast ahead, writes another quidem, which is answered by sed, "these things must be manifest, but they must not be flaunted." The second quidem therefore has a double value: looking back to the earlier sentence, to which it forms the antithesis, it is Adversative; looking ahead, it as at the same time Contrasting.

Contrasting plus Adversative quidem. Even without a preceding quidem, quidem may look in both directions and appear either Contrasting or Adversative. sed magnum nescioquid necessest evenisse, Parmeno, unde ira inter eas intercessit quae tam permansit diu. --haud quidem hercle: parvom; si vis vero veram rationem exsequi . . ., Ter.Hec.306;

quidem is Adversative (it opposes haud to magnum) and at the same time Contrasting (it looks forward to si vis vero); there is therefore no need to alter the MSS. and read with Bentley aut quidem. (the speaker is urging the Gauls to show at least as much bravery against the Romans as they once had against the Cimbri) depopulata Gallia Cimbri magnaque inlata calamitate finibus quidem nostris aliquando excesserunt atque alias terras petiverunt; iura leges agros libertatem nobis reliquerunt. Romani vero quid petunt aliud aut quid volunt, nisi invidia adducti, quos fama nobilis potentisque bello cognoverunt, horum in agris civitatibusque considere atque his aeternam iniungere servitutem? Caes.Gal. 7.77.14. Quidem may be understood, with Grossmann, p. 17, as Adversative, marking the second member of a contrast, the members of which are not grammatically parallel; quidem then would oppose the main clause to the preceding ablative absolutes; we might paraphrase this "they wrought great havoc; they did, however, depart." But quidem may also be Contrasting, setting in opposition the Cimbri and the Romans, "the Cimbri left, but the Romans want to settle here forever." On this view the position of quidem is odd--Cimbri quidem would have been clearer--but depopulata Gallia . . . magnaque inlata calamitate may be intended to apply to the Romans also: "After devastating Gaul, the Cimbri . . . but the Romans . . ." This would be the only Contrasting quidem in Caesar. But Meusel, who in his critical appendix defends

the preservation of quidem, which is omitted by a family of
MSS., proposes a third way of taking quidem, as a Contrasting
quidem solum: finibus excesserunt is opposed to iura, leges
. . . reliquerunt, "they departed from our territory but
left us our laws, etc." On balance this last seems to me
most probable. The claims of Contrasting and Adversative
quidem are more even in the next two passages. se eis dumtaxat vitam concessurum; bona quidem eorum se venditurum,
ita tamen . . ., B.Afr.90.1; either "would spare them but
sell their property" (Adversative) or "would, to be sure,
sell their property, yet in such a way . . ." (Contrasting).
in eloquendo est aliqua diversitas (sc. inter Demosthenem et
Ciceronem) . . . in epistulis quidem, quamquam sunt utrius-
que, dialogisve, quibus nihil ille, nulla contentio est.
cedendum vero in hoc, quod et prior fuit et ex magna parte
Ciceronem quantus est fecit, Quint.10.1.107; either quidem
is Adversative and opposes writings to speeches or quidem is
Contrasting and balances Cicero's superiority against the
fact that Demosthenes was first and in large measure made
Cicero's achievement possible.

Contrasting plus Extending quidem. As Contrasting quidem sometimes overlaps with Adversative, so too does it
overlap with Extending on occasion. ex me quaerunt . . .
-- quaerunt quidem, C. Laeli, multi, ut est a Fannio dictum,
sed ego id respondeo quod animum adverti, Cic.Amic.8. The
reader, as his eye moves along, most naturally will take

quidem to be the common Extending sort which picks up a word from the previous speaker, "many do indeed ask" (see pp. 111-112). But when the following clause begins it appears that the quidem was also Contrasting. Exactly the same ambiguity is present in the following two passages. "mihi quidem Antiochum, quem audis, satis belle videris attendere." tum ille timide vel potius verecunde, "facio" inquit "equidem; sed audistine modo de Carneade? rapior illuc," Fin.5.6, where the quidem after mihi is Emphatic or Limiting and the equidem is both Extending and Contrasting. "non patiar" inquit; "causam enim tollam." et ego: "rectissime quidem; sed si grave non est, velim scire quid sit causae," Att. 13.42.1. at multis se probavit (sc. Epicurus). et quidem iure fortasse, sed tamen non gravissimum est testimonium multitudinis, Fin.2.81. convenerunt conrogati, et quidem ampli quidam homines, sed immemores dignitatis suae, Phil. 3.20. vestrum iam hic factum deprehenditur, patres conscripti, non meum, ac pulcherrimum quidem factum, verum, ut dixi, non meum, sed vestrum, Cic.ap.Quint.9.3.40.

Sometimes quidem appears to be used in both halves of a contrast. magnos quidem viros, maiores quidem quia in laudem vetustorum invidia non obstat, Sen.Ben.7.8.2, "great men indeed, but all the greater because envy is no bar to the praise of the ancients;" unless we alter the text--Madvig deleted the first quidem, Koch proposed quondam in its place--the first quidem seems to be Contrasting and the second Adversative, as Ludewig notes, p. 68; the second might also be considered Extending. Another possible Senecan example is: cetera opinione bona sunt et nomen quidem habent commune cum veris, proprietas quidem in illis boni non est, Ep.74.17; editors regularly sacrifice the second quidem, though the first would be an equally acceptable victim and though the previous example in fact supports keeping both quidems here. The text of Cicero offers another possible example. ac separatim quidem, quae de principio et de insinuatione dicenda videbantur, haec fere sunt: nunc quidem brevi communiter de utroque praecipiendum videtur, Inv. 1.25; the MSS. have quidem and quidam, Stroebel reads a sensible quiddam.

Now in all these passages the problem is essentially the same: the uncertainty of quidem's other reference. I have defined quidem as a word that emphasizes one thing by reference to another and have described five categories of use, in which the "other" stands in different relations to quidem. It is the very uncertainty as to what the other reference is that makes these passages ambiguous. As Seyffert well remarks (ad Cic.Amic.24): "ob ein Gegensatz folgt, vorhergeht, oder gar nicht vorhanden ist, ist für die Bedeutung von quidem gleichgültig." We should not then regard these ambiguities as violations of quidem's nature or toyings with it, but rather as its natural consequence.

Here may be seen the difference between my explanation

of _quidem_ and those given by Grossmann and Ludewig, for example. In explaining the _quidem_s in such passages they would be forced to choose from their various categories; and, since little exists in common to all their categories, they could choose no more than one, thus losing any possibility of an accurate explanation. Let us note that the passages we were examining are not transitional. Though often, as we shall see later, a _quidem_ does lie between two categories, as, for instance, between Limiting and Emphatic or between Adversative and Extending, here it does not; the _quidem_ serves two distinct purposes at the same time.

A practical problem arises here: as we read along how do we recognize the _quidem_s we meet? how do we tell whether the _quidem_ looks back or forward? In fact we often cannot recognize the use of _quidem_ at first glance, but this is not so serious a difficulty as it may seem, and it can be attacked in several ways. One may explain it away by arguing that if we today did not need to look for a suitable equivalent in our own language, the difficulty would disappear; to us it may be "on the one hand" or "however" or "indeed," but to the Romans it was just _quidem_. This solution is too simple. The practical difficulty is real but, I would say, no greater than with other words. When we read the words _et Cicero_, can we be immediately certain that they mean "and Cicero," not "even Cicero" or "both Cicero" (implying a correlative _et_)? Does a _quod_ at the beginning of a sentence mean "because" or "that which?" Such examples make me doubt whether any special difficulty attaches to recognizing the force of a particular quidem.

It is convenient to restate here three important features of quidem which will meet us again in the following sections. 1. Quidem corresponds frequently to the Greek particle μέν. 2. Quidem is strongly attracted to pronouns, even contrary to logic. 3. Though attached to one word, quidem often emphasizes the whole clause.

I.B. Contrasting *quidem* *solum*

Contrasting *quidem* without a following adversative scarcely differs from contrasting *quidem* with. Indeed these examples might simply have been included in the preceding section; but the present arrangement, though implying too large a distinction, will, I hope, more firmly establish this use of *quidem*, which has received scant attention, despite its frequency.

The contrast, lacking an adversative, tends to be marked neatly and clearly by the words themselves. The same is true in Greek when μέν is not followed by a particle; Denniston, p. 377, notes that "by far the commonest type" is πρῶτον μέν . . . ἔπειτα. The obviousness of the contrast makes an adversative superfluous. tu quidem, inquit, rex, deos quaeso, perpetua felicitate floreas: ego ceteris laetus hoc uno torqueor, Curt.6.5.3. ille quidem, qui collegam et generum adsciverat, sibi ignoscit; ceteri, quem per dedecora fovere, cum scelere insectantur, Tac.Ann.5.6. utrum enim horum dixeris, in eo culpa et crimen haerebit. nam illud quidem non dices . . . hoc tu feres? hoc quisquam defendet? Cic.Ver.3.107. atque antea quidem maiores copias alere poterat; nunc exiguas vix tueri potest, Deiot.22. consul . . . suos quidem a fuga revocavit, ipse . . . missili traiectus cecidit, Liv.41.18.11; Weissenborn-Müller: "*suos* steht *ipse* entgegen."

The lack of an adversative also tends to make the units short, lest the reader lose sight of the contrast. Longer examples are rare. nunc quidem proficiscentem ad comparationem frumentorum Maximum libertum meum recte militibus instruxisti. fungebatur enim et ipse extraordinario munere. cum ad pristinum actum reversus fuerit, sufficient illi duo a te dati milites, Traj. in Plin.Ep.10.28, where nunc and cum are contrasted.

Here, as with ordinary Contrasting quidem, we see a similar but weaker tendency for quidem to be displaced next to a pronoun. at hi quidem, ut populi Romani aetas est, senes, ut Atheniensium saecula numerantur, adulescentes debent videri, Cic.Brut.39, instead of ut quidem or senes quidem. quem quidem sui Caesarem salutabant, Philippus non, Att.14.12.2, instead of sui quidem. illos quidem merito perisse ipsorum maleficio ait, victuros suo atque populi Romani beneficio, Liv.28.34.8. et hic quidem prius dictus est Varus, post Heliogabalus, S.H.A.Eleg.1.6, in place of prius quidem.

We see the same possibility for contrast between nonparallel units. debitos nato quidem compesce fletus, Sen. Her.O.1832, quidem going with the phrase debitos nato, "though they are owed to a son, restrain them." sine hac quidem constantia ipsa illa ex tempore dicendi facultas inanem modo loquacitatem dabit, Quint.10.3.2, where hac constantia is contrasted with illa facultas; Peterson's conscientia spoils the contrast. saliunca folio quidem subbrevi et quod necti non possit, radici numerosae cohaeret, Plin. Nat.21.43, "though its leaves are quite short, it has a large network of roots;" Mayhoff suggests, however, that the original, now mutilated, may have been something like lato quidem sed brevi. et Maximo quidem ad bellum profecto Romae praetoriani remanserunt, S.H.A.Max.Balb.9.1.

We also see this quidem used for rounding off one section and beginning another. ac de inductione quidem satis in praesentia dictum videtur. nunc deinceps ratiocinationis vim et naturam consideremus, Cic.Inv.1.56. et de arboribus quidem fructus gratia serendis inserendisque in universum sint dicta haec. restat earum ratio quae propter alias seruntur, Plin.Nat.17.140. With equidem. verum haec ipse equidem spatiis exclusus iniquis praetereo atque aliis post me memoranda relinquo. nunc age, naturas apibus quas Iuppiter ipse addidit expediam, Verg.G.4.147 (some inferior MSS. read quidem).

Finally Contrasting quidem solum shows the same ability as Contrasting quidem to join things which are not really opposed to one another. In the first passage, the quidem clause serves mainly as a foil to the other; in the second and third, both clauses are balanced rather than opposed. omnes quidem laeti, ante alios Thracum insolens laetitia eminebat, Liv.42.60.2. qua aut terra aut mari persequar eum qui ubi sit nescio? etsi terra quidem qui possum? mari quo? Cic.Att.7.22.2. equitatus quidem cessit, duces caetratae cohortis . . . occasionem bene gerendae rei amisere, Liv.31.36.3.

Examples of Contrasting quidem solum. nequaquam argenti ratio comparet tamen. -- ratio quidem hercle apparet: argentum οἴχεται , Plaut.Trin.419, "the account seems okay; it's the money that's gone." ill' quidem hanc abducet; tu nullus adfueris, si non lubet, Bac.90. puerum accipias; nam is quidem in culpa non est: post de matre videro, Ter.Hec. 699. nam de pueritia quidem tua, quam tu omnium intemperantiae addixisti, dicerem, si hoc tempus idoneum putarem: nunc consulto relinquo, Rhet.Her.4.37. ac de exordio quidem satis dictum est. narratio est rerum gestarum aut ut gestarum expositio, Cic.Inv.1.26. et apud Graecos quidem iam anni prope quadringenti sunt cum hoc probatur; nos nuper agnovimus, Orat.171. maiores quidem nostri non modo ut liberi essent sed etiam ut imperarent, arma capiebant: tu arma abicienda censes ut serviamus? Phil.8.12. quae quidem (sc. tua vita) quae miretur iam pridem multa habet; nunc etiam quae laudet exspectat, Marc.28; quidem is displaced next to the pronoun, but contrasts miretur with laudet. magnamque Graeciam, quae nunc quidem deleta est, tum florebat, institutis et praeceptis suis erudierunt, Amic.13. accusabat autem ille quidem Scamandrum verbis tribus VENENUM EST DEPREHENSUM; omnia tela totius accusationis in Oppianicum coniciebantur, Clu.50. Peterson's note is excellent: "Ille quidem restricts and contrasts: tr. 'but while he limited his impeachment of Scamander to the three words POISON WAS DISCOVERED, it was against Oppianicus that the whole artillery of the prosecution was directed.' . . . The word here intimates an antithesis, which follows asyndetically;" he also mentions the tendency of quidem to be juxtaposed with personal pronouns when really affecting the whole sentence. quam cito tu istinc cupias, nescio; ego quidem eo magis, quo adhuc felicius res gessisti, dum istic eris, de belli Parthi periculo cruciabor, Cael.Fam.8.7.1. sibi quidem persuaderi . . . eum neque suam neque populi Romani gratiam repudiaturum. quodsi furore atque amentia impulsus bellum intulisset, quid tandem vererentur?, Caes.Gal.1.40.3; this is one of the few instances of Contrasting quidem solum in Caesar (another is Civ.3.74.2); of Contrasting there appear to be no instances, except perhaps in the problematic passage Gal. 7.77.14 (see above, pp. 61-62). illa quidem (sc. Eurydice) Stygia nabat iam frigida cumba. septem illum (sc. Orphea) totos perhibent ex ordine mensis rupe sub aëria deserti ad Strymonis undam flesse sibi, Verg.G.4.506. et nunc ille quidem (sc. Evander) spe multum captus inani fors et vota facit cumulatque altaria donis, nos iuvenem exanimum et nil iam caelestibus ullis debentem vano maesti comitamur honore, A.11.49.

et tum quidem ab nocturno iuvenali ludo in castra redeunt. paucis interiectis diebus Sex. Tarquinius . . . Collatiam venit, Liv.1.57.11. ego quidem nulli vestrum deero; ne fortuna mea desit videte, 6.18.8. et ceteras quidem (sc. civitates) . . . haud difficulter videbat iugum accepturas: Zmyrna et Lampsacus libertatem usurpabant, 33.38.2. exerceri quidem illo volebat, gloriari fastidiebat, Sen.Con.4. pref.2. digna quidem facies, pro qua vel obiret Achilles; vel Priamo belli causa probanda fuit. si quis vult fama tabulas anteire vetustas, hic dominam exemplo ponat in arte meam, Prop.2.3.39. Polyperconti quidem postea custodito diu ignovit: in Callisthenem olim contumacia suspectum pervicacioris irae fuit, Curt.8.6.1. ac primo quidem quae sit forma totius, quae maximae partes, quo singulae modo sint atque habitentur expediam, deinde rursus oras omnium et litora . . ., Mela 1.2.

qui dedit, gratiam quidem iam recepit, mercedem nondum, Sen.Ben.2.33.3. Aegyptium quidem tale, alterius nationis contritum splendescit ut misy et est lapidosius, Plin.Nat. 34.120. ille quidem pensabat iter propiusque secabat aera, si medias Europae scinderet urbes: Pallas frugiferas iussit non laedere terras et parci populis, Luc.9.685. ira feras quidem mentes obsidet, eruditas praelabitur, Petr.99.3. utinam quidem hac se inscriptione maculassent: haberemus nos extremum solacium. nunc mimicis artibus petiti sumus et adumbrata inscriptione derisi, Petr.106.1. utinam quidem iam tenerentur omnia et in aperto confessa veritas esset nihilque ex decretis mutaremus! nunc veritatem cum eis ipsis qui docent quaerimus, Sen.<u>Dial</u>.8.3.1. With the two preceding examples compare this passage: utinam quidem fuissem! molestus nobis non esset. sed hoc vestrum est, Cic.<u>Fam</u>. 12.3.1, which well illustrates how close Contrasting <u>quidem solum</u> is to ordinary Contrasting. et scriptor quidem semper tueri signatorem necesse habet, signator scriptorem non semper, Quint.7.2.53. et M. Tullius inventionem quidem ac dispositionem prudentis hominis putat, eloquentiam oratoris, 8.pref.14. ipse quidem malit terras pugnatque reverti, fert ingens a puppe Notus, Stat.<u>Theb</u>.3.28.

suasoriae quidem . . . pueris delegantur, controversiae robustioribus adsignantur, Tac.<u>Dial</u>.35.4. et eques quidem scuto frameaque contentus est, pedites et missilia spargunt, <u>Germ</u>.6.1. et nox quidem . . . proximus dies . . ., <u>Agr</u>. 38.1; nine short clauses precede the second half of the contrast; Kritz says: "<u>quidem</u> additum, quo <u>nox</u> distinctius opponatur <u>diei proximo</u>." illum quidem sua maiestas, imperium Romanum ceteri exercitus defendent, <u>Ann</u>.1.42. et circa Classicum quidem brevis et expeditus labor . . . circa Hispanum et Probum multum sudoris, Plin.<u>Ep</u>.3.9.12. et haec quidem adfirmantibus credo; illud adfirmare aliis possum, <u>Ep</u>.7.27.12. nomine quidem flumen, re vera cloaca foedissima, <u>Ep</u>.10.98.1. (quoting Claudius) alteram quidem brevem et innoxiam, alteram non iniustam fore, Suet.<u>Cl</u>.38.1. duo vero sapientissimos et clarissimos fratres P. Crassum et P. Scaevolam aiunt Tib. Graccho legum auctores fuisse, alterum quidem ut videmus palam, alterum ut suspicantur obscurius, Cic. Luc.13. et illas quidem divitias publicae custodelae commisere, Tlepolemo puellam repetitam lege tradidere, Apul. Met.7.13 (Plasberg's Tlepolemo ⟨vero⟩ is unnecessary). pelices nunc quidem appellantur alienis succumbentes non solum feminae, sed etiam mares. antiqui proprie eam pelicem nominabant, quae uxorem habenti nubebat, Paul.Fest. p. 248 L. prima quidem haec caligo, dehinc post terra creata est, spirantum sedes firmissima, pectore vasto, Chalcidius poet. 8, translating Hes.Theog.116: ἤτοι μὲν πρώτιστα χάος γένετ', αὐτὰρ ἔπειτα εὐρύστερνος πάντων ἕδος ἀσφαλὲς αἰεί.

Contrasting equidem solum. nam Fauni vocem equidem numquam audivi; tibi, si audivisse te dicis, credam, Cic. N.D.3.15. quae tum significatio fuerit omnium . . . equidem audiebam, existimare facilius possunt qui adfuerunt, Ses. 122. equidem me Caesaris militem dici volui, vos me imperatoris nomine appellavistis, Caes.Civ.2.32.13, the only equidem in Caesar except perhaps for orat.27 (on which see above, p. 26). non equidem invideo, miror magis, Verg.Ecl. 1.11. hoc equidem occasum Troiae tristisque ruinas solabar . . . nunc eadem fortuna viros tot casibus actos insequitur, A.1.238. abolere propere pessimam ferro luem equidem parabam: precibus evicit gener, Sen.Med.184. vellem equidem nostri tetigissent litora patris te sine duxque illis alius quicumque fuisset. nunc remeant, Val.Flac.8.432.

II. Adversative quidem

The use of quidem in the second half of a contrast has been called Adversative. This term, though adopted here, may be misleading, for it attributes to quidem a force that it does not properly have and conceals the relation of this use to the others, especially to Contrasting quidem. As Grossmann well says, p. 104: "Sed ea vis (sc. adversativa) plerumque non particulae 'quidem' tribuenda est, sed rebus in sententiis exstantibus, quae quidem sibi oppositae sunt, ut 'quidem' rem alteram altera magis commemorans, oppositione sine particula praemissa idem atque 'autem' significet." Consequently it is not illogical to combine quidem with an adversative, even though in effect both do the same job of pointing back. benigne edepol facis. -- immo tu quidem hercle vero, Plaut.Rud.1369. aer dissaepit collis atque aera montes, terra mare et contra mare terras terminat omnis; omne quidem vero nil est quod finiat extra, Lucr.1.987 (1001).

It is more useful and accurate to regard Adversative quidem as the reverse of Contrasting quidem; quidem now glances back instead of forwards. The Greek particle μέν is also used in the second limb of a contrast (Denniston, pp. 377-78), though far less often than quidem is so used. The closeness of Adversative to Contrasting quidem may be seen from a pair of passages in Pliny the Elder. reliqua huius sinus dicantur, et maria quidem eius nuncupavimus,

Nat.4.91. Here the order of the clauses is reversed from the regular idiom, in which first a _quidem_ clause summarizes the preceding, and then a following clause brings us to the next topic; we may compare: et maria quidem gentesque . . . ad hunc modum se habent, insulae autem . . ., 4.52. In the following passage Pliny reverses, not the clauses, but only the particle: (passing from alimentary to medicinal uses of plants) et hactenus hortensia dicta sint ciborum gratia dumtaxat. maximum quidem opus in iisdem naturae restat, 19.189. Both passages illustrate the ease with which Contrasting and Adversative _quidem_ can be interchanged.

It is natural for the second member, since it does come second and is marked by _quidem_, to be emphasized more than the first, as a glance at the examples will suggest. Out of this tendency are bred many of the overlappings between Adversative _quidem_ and Emphatic, Limiting, and Extending _quidem_.

Even more than Contrasting, Adversative _quidem_ is liable to be found with non-parallel syntactic elements, main clause with relative clause and protasis with apodosis being the most common combinations. quod fortasse aliquando universae rei publicae nostrae, nunc quidem profecto isti provinciae contigit, Cic.Q.fr.1.1.29, "what once may have befallen the whole state, now for sure has befallen that province." Cotta, qui se valde dilatandis litteris a similitudine Graecae locutionis abstraxerat sonabatque contrarium

Catulo, subagreste quiddam planeque subrusticum, alia quidem quasi inculta et silvestri via ad eandem laudem pervenerat, Brut.259, "though different from Catulus, yet he achieved the same glory." haec ille, si verbis non audet, re quidem vera palam loquitur, Quinct.56. si non statim, paulo quidem post, Quinct.40. ad me ventum est qui, ut summa haberem cetera, temporis quidem certe vix satis habui, Quinct.3. interdixit histrionibus scaenam, intra domum quidem exercendi artem iure concesso, Suet.Dom.7.1.

Again like Contrasting quidem, Adversative can be used when two notions are to be linked rather than opposed to one another. cruciatus est a Dolabella Trebonius: et quidem a Carthaginiensibus Regulus, Phil.11.9. mearum epistularum nulla est συναγωγή; sed habet Tiro instar septuaginta, et quidem sunt a te quaedam sumendae, Att.16.5.5.

Most often the units are short, with quidem following, and thereby setting off, the contrasting word in the second unit. quas leges ausus est non nemo improbus, potuit quidem nemo convellere, Cic.Pis.10; Nisbet translates "laws which some wretch may have boldly attempted, but none has been able, to tear down," and then adds that "in sense, though not in form, the first clause is subordinate to the second." verbo ille reus erat, re quidem vera et periculo tota accusatione Oppianicus, Clu.54, " λόγῳ μέν . . . ἔργῳ δέ" (Peterson). nocere itaque nobis possunt . . . iniuriam quidem facere non possunt, Sen.Dial.4.26.4, "harm they can do us, injury they cannot." Less commonly the contrasting parts are more separated. elegia quoque Graecos provocamus . . . (brief mention of Tibullus, Propertius, Ovid, and Gallus) satura quidem tota nostra est, Quint.10.1.93, "in elegy we rival the Greeks, but in satire there is no competition." prima iuventa variorum dedecorum infamiam subiit. (Four sentences, of 71 words altogether, report various allegations of homosexuality.) adulteria quidem exercuisse ne amici quidem negant, Suet.Aug.68. (for almost a page dialectic, one of the three divisions of philosophy, has been under discussion) iam quidem pars illa moralis quae dicitur Ethice, certe tota oratori est accomodata, Quint.12.2.15; the contrast with dialectic is distant and weak.

Examples of Adversative quidem. in foro palam omnis vendo pro meis venalibus. mare quidem commune certost omnibus, Plaut.Rud.975. di te perdant! -- vos quidem hercle, Poen.588, "God damn you! -- No, you rather." illius avia. -- immo mater quidem, Cis.515. laborem utilem studiosis, mihi quidem ipsi non necessarium, Cic.Opt.Gen.13. hoc (sc. Dianae simulacrum) translatum Carthaginem locum tantum hominesque mutarat, religionem quidem pristinam conservabat, Ver.4.72. causa cognita possunt multi absolvi, incognita quidem condemnari nemo potest, Ver.1.25. iacet ille nunc prostratus, Quirites, et se perculsum atque abiectum esse sentit et retorquet oculos profecto saepe ad hanc urbem quam e suis faucibus ereptam esse luget: quae quidem mihi laetari videtur, quod tantam pestem evomuerit forasque proiecerit, Catil.2.2, "and yet the city . . . ." quid enim quisquam potest ex omni memoria sumere inlustrius quam pro uno civi et bonos omnis privato consensu et universum senatum publico consilio mutasse vestem? quae quidem tum mutatio non deprecationis est causa facta, sed luctus, Ses.27, "yet this change of raiment . . .;" Adversative quidem with the relative is common in Cicero. quae (sc. res communes) quales sint, non facile est scribere. sunt quidem certe in amicorum nostrorum potestate, Fam.1.8.1. cogitatione inter se differunt, re quidem copulata sunt, Tusc.4.24. omnes id agamus ut haec quam primum in omnes ordines quaestio perferatur. interea quidem, per deos immortales!, Clu.155, an elliptic example. P. Lucceium mihi meum commendas; quem quibuscumque rebus potero diligenter tuebor. Hirtium quidem et Pansam, conlegas nostros, homines in consulatu rei p. salutaris, alieno sane tempore amisimus, Fam.12.25a.6; the contrast is rather weak, "I will look after Lucceius, but we've already lost Hirtius and Pansa, the consuls."

tanta subito malacia ac tranquillitas exstitit ut se ex loco commovere non possent. quae quidem res ad negotium conficiendum maxime fuit opportuna, Caes.Gal.3.15.4, "they were becalmed, and yet this turned out to be to their advantage." praeoccupatum sese legatione ab Cn. Pompeio teneri obstrictum fide; necessitudinem quidem sibi nihilo minorem cum Caesare intercedere, Civ.2.17.2; Adversative quidem is relatively common in Caesar. hunc adversus Pharnabazus habitus est imperator, re quidem vera exercitui praefuit Conon, Nep.Con.2.2. haec igitur possent utendi cognita causa credier, ex usu quae sunt vitaque reperta. illa quidem sorsum sunt omnia quae prius ipsa nata dedere suae post notitiam utilitatis, Lucr.4.853. quem non super occupat Hisbo, ille quidem hoc sperans, Verg.A.10.385, "Hisbo did not catch him, though he was hoping to."

tu tamen iniecta tectus, vesane, lacerna potabis galea fessus Araxis aquam. illa quidem interea fama tabescet inani, Prop.3.12.9. at nunc a puero Thebae capientur inermi, quem neque bella iuvant nec tela nec usus equorum . . . quem quidem ego actutum (modo vos absistite) cogam assumptumque patrem commentaque sacra fateri, Ov.Met.3.557. nam, quia dentibus carent, aut lambunt cibos aut integros hauriunt; mandare quidem non possunt, Colum.8.17.11. illum ego feliciorem dixerim qui nihil negotii secum habuit, hunc quidem melius de se meruisse qui malignitatem naturae suae vicit, Sen.Ep.52.6. omnes enim inter se differant, sapiens quidem pares illos ob aequalem stultitiam omnis putat, Dial.2.13.5. corpora obnoxia sunt et adscripta dominis, mens quidem sui iuris, Ben.3.20.1. istuc nobis licet dicere, vobis quidem non licet, Ep.99.28. Seneca, as Ludewig, p. 66, points out, was especially fond of Adversative quidem, which permits a pointed antithesis to take the reader by surprise. Attico haec quoque (sc. umbra ulmorum) videtur e gravissimis, nec dubito, si emittantur in ramos; constrictae quidem illius noxiam esse non arbitror, Plin.Nat.17.90. deteriores in agris pinguibus (sc. nasci), veram quidem dictamnum non nisi in asperis, Nat.25.93. adulteratur (sc. piper) iuniperi bacis mire vim trahentibus, in pondere quidem multis modis, Nat.12.29.

pugna fuit, non longa quidem, Luc.4.472. in foro quoque contingere istud principiorum genus secundis actionibus potest, primis quidem raro umquam, Quint.4.1.4. omnibus (sc. figuris) scriptores sua nomina dederunt, sed varia et ut cuique fingenti placuit: fons quidem unus, 9.3.54. nam rebus atrocibus verba etiam ipso auditu aspera magis conveniunt. in universum quidem optima simplicium creduntur quae aut maxime exclamant aut sono sunt iucundissima. et honesta quidem turpibus potiora semper, 8.3.17; each quidem marks an objection to the original proposition. si cunctatione deliqui, virtute corrigam. vestra quidem vis et gloria in integro est, Tac.Ann.15.2. plausus tantum ac potius sola cymbala et tympana . . . desunt: ululatus quidem . . . large supersunt, Plin.Ep.2.14.13. hebetentur fortasse et paulum retundantur, evelli quidem extorquerique non possunt, Ep.3.15.4. frigidissimos versus esse dicebat, omnium quidem iudicio venustissimos, Gel.7.16.2.

Examples of Adversative equidem. insania. -- equidem sana sum, Plaut.Am.720; "It's insane. -- But I'm quite sane." nondum scis. -- scio equidem illam ducturum esse te, Ter.An.659. vos haec melius scire potestis, equidem audita dico, Cic.Ses.72. de timore supervacuaneum est disserere . . . de poena possum equidem dicere, Sal.Cat.51.20. servati consulis decus Coelius ad servum natione Ligurem delegat; malim equidem de filio verum esse quod et plures tradidere auctores et fama obtinuit, Liv.21.46.10.

Partial concession. One particular use of Adversative quidem deserves separate notice. This is the use of quidem to confirm the preceding statement and at the same time to offer another which in part undermines the first. "Yes, but" or "and yet" will serve as translations. Seyffert describes it so: "Dieselbe Form (sc. et quidem) wird nun aber auch ad infirmandam aut dissolvendam adversarii sententiam, indem ich zu derselben etwas hinzufüge, was mit ihr in Widerspruch steht, was sie beschränkt oder umstösst."[26] Seyffert, by the way, like Grossmann, who quotes him on p. 107, and others, is hindered by the formal fallacy and fails to see that the et is inessential, the work being done by quidem; none of them sufficiently appreciated the note by Madvig (ad Cic.Fin.1.35), who not only first described this use but also offered examples both with quidem and with et quidem.

[26] Moritz Seyffert, Scholae Latinae, pt. 1, 3rd ed. (Leipzig, 1870), p. 158; see also his note on Cic.Amic.79.

This use is often found in Cicero, occasionally in Seneca and elsewhere. The tone is often, but not invariably, ironic. est enim vis tanta naturae ut homo nemo velit nisi hominis similis esse. et quidem formica formicae, Cic.N.D. 1.79; Mayor's description of the idiom is excellent: "This formula is often used to express an ironical acceptance of an opponent's argument, professing to carry it further but really showing that it is applicable in an opposite sense to that intended by the user." The next example is not ironic: at in ipsum Habitum animadverterunt. nullam quidem ob turpitudinem, Clu.133; "'Yes, but not for,' etc. Quidem is here used to lessen the force of the preceding statement" (Peterson). "causam enim" inquit "cognosci oportet." ea re quidem, quod aliter condemnari reus, quamvis sit nocens, non potest, Ver.1.25, "The case, he says, ought to be carried on. Yes, I agree, but his reason is that in no other way can the defendant be convicted," i.e. don't believe his claim to be seeking justice. "at aliquando inceditur (sc. populus a tribunis plebis)." et quidem saepe sedatur, Leg. 3.24, "'But the populace is sometimes aroused by them.' And yet it is often calmed by them." "est enim turpe iudicium." ex facto quidem turpi, Caec.8, "'It is a disgraceful judgment.' True, but the action was disgraceful." "at laudat saepe virtutem." et quidem C. Gracchus, cum largitiones maximas fecisset et effudisset aerarium, verbis tamen defendebat aerarium, Tusc.3.48; "The argument is 'It may be urged that Epicurus often praises virtue. True, but men's words are not always in harmony with their deeds. C. Gracchus praised economy while squandering the public treasure'" (Dougan). "at Phalaris, at Apollodorus poenas sustulit." multis quidem ante cruciatis et necatis, N.D.3.82. "torquem detraxit hosti." et quidem se texit, ne interiret. "at magnum periculum adiit." in oculis quidem exercitus, Fin. 1.35. rarum genus! et quidem omnia praeclara rara, Amic. 79; see Seyffert. multum, inquit, viva vox facit. non quidem haec quae alienis verbis commodatur et actuari vice fungitur, Sen.Ep.33.9. "terribiles visu formae, Letumque Labosque." minime quidem, si quis rectius oculis intueri illa possit et tenebras perrumpere, Ep.104.24. fassu' s Charmidem dedisse aurum tibi. -- scriptum quidem, Plaut.Trin.982; Gray (ad 971) explains: "scriptum quidem corrects and limits his statement that Charmides had given him the money, 'at any rate (if he had not given the cash) he had given an order for it.'"

Transitional examples. After these examples of ordinary Adversative quidem it is worthwhile to look at some others which suggest its interconnection and overlap with the other uses. Though obviously akin to Contrasting quidem, of which it is nothing other than the reverse, Adversative quidem can rarely overlap with it, since one quidem looks forward, the other backward; some of the few instances where _quidem_ appears to look in both directions are collected above, pp. 60-62. With Emphatic, Limiting, and Extending _quidem_, however, Adversative has closer ties. Unlike Contrasting _quidem_, the parts of which tend to be of equal weight, in Adversative the second part, the one containing _quidem_, carries greater weight. Adversative _quidem_ therefore more nearly approaches both Extending, in which the second part rises above the first, and Emphatic and Limiting, in which the other part is not present and needs to be supplied mentally.

Adversative-Extending _quidem_. To the extent that the second element in Adversative _quidem_ becomes more prominent than the first and moves beyond it to a stronger statement, it comes closer to Extending _quidem_. et soletis queri; Zeno quidem etiam litigabat, Cic.N.D.1.93, "you usually complain; Zeno, however, even went to law." Zeno is contrasted with the "you" of soletis, but his protest goes beyond theirs, as if to say "and what is more, Zeno . . ." The word _etiam_ points to the greater intensity of the second statement, but even without a pointer we would see that _litigare_ is stronger that _queri_. This passage reminds us that _quidem_ does not itself mean "and, what is more" but rather joins thoughts which stand in this relation to one another. (In the same way, the two passages on p. 75 with both _quidem_ and an adversative in the second half showed that _quidem_ did not in itself have an adversative force.)

ego ne Torquatum quidem illum qui hoc cognomen invenit iratum existimo Gallo torquem detraxisse. . . . de Africano quidem, quia notior est nobis propter recentem memoriam, vel iurare possum non illum iracundia tum inflammatum fuisse, cum . . ., Cic.<u>Tusc</u>.4.50; Dougan well observes that "<u>quidem</u> . . . lends emphasis to the word preceding: the emphasis here serves to contrast the necessarily conjectural statement (<u>existimo</u>) about Torquatus with the vigorous certainty (<u>vel iurare possum</u>) of the expression about Scipio." ipsum Scipionem accepimus non infantem fuisse. filius quidem eius . . . si corpore valuisset, in primis habitus esset disertus, <u>Brut</u>.77. me amicissime cotidie magis Caesar amplectitur, familiares quidem eius sicuti neminem, <u>Fam</u>.6.6.13, where the context makes it clear that the second half means "are fonder of me than of any one else." est enim finitimus oratori poeta, numeris adstrictior paulo, verborum autem licentia liberior, multis vero ornandi generibus socius ac paene par; in hoc quidem certe prope idem, nullis ut terminis circumscribat aut definiat ius suum, de <u>Orat</u>.1.70, "a partner and near equal--practically identical;" Wilkins is wrong to claim that "<u>quidem</u> has become merely an enclitic of emphasis, so that <u>certe</u> is not redundant." (after discussing the attacks Phaedrus and Epicurus made on their opponents) Zeno quidem non eos solum qui tum erant . . . figebat maledictis, sed Socraten ipsum parentem philosophiae . . . scurram Atticum fuisse dicebat, <u>N.D</u>.1.93, i.e. Zeno went far beyond the others in the sharpness of his attacks. nihil cupide agemus, sine tuo quidem consilio certe nihil, Att.6.3.3. hunc amor, ira quidem communiter urit utrumque, Hor.Ep.1.2.13. thelyphronon omnem quadripedem necat inposita verendis radice, folio quidem intra eundem diem, Plin.Nat.25.122, "thelyphronon kills every quadruped when the root is applied to its genitals; indeed, when the leaf is applied it kills them within the same day." vetaretque loqui aut agere quicquam nisi propalam et quod in diurnos commentarios referretur; extraneorum quidem coetu adeo prohibuit ut . . ., Suet.Aug.64.2. est quod ego tecum graviter conquerar, mi magister, et quidem ut querelam dolor superet, Fro.Ver.2.p.294 (116N). (See also pp. 118-119 for more examples.)

Adversative-Emphatic quidem. Emphatic quidem implies a reference to something else: "he is not happy (though perhaps we or you or they are)." In true Emphatic quidem the contrasting element is only implied, not directly mentioned. There are, however, many instances in which the contrasting element is mentioned in a preceding sentence (and so the quidem is Adversative), but is mentioned in so skewed or casual a fashion that the quidem seems as much Emphatic as Adversative. The contrast itself is not the main point; often it is only loosely conceived or carried out. The result is a slight vagueness; the reader, not grasping at once the contrast marked by quidem, feels its force to be confined to the word or phrase that accompanies it. That is to say, the feebler the contrast with what precedes, the closer Adversative comes to Emphatic quidem.

This kind of quidem, located between Adversative and Emphatic, is very common, and I give many examples. inveneris. ex me quidem hodie numquam fies certior, Plaut. Bac.841; there is a latent contrast, "you'll find out, but you'll never learn anything from me," but quidem presses with most of its weight on the word me. immo in carcerem; nam hic quidem genium meliorem tuom non facies, St.622. di melius faxint! -- di hoc quidem faciunt, Mer.285, "May the gods treat you better! -- But the gods do treat me better;" quidem, though displaced next to the pronoun, emphasizes the truth of the whole clause, which emphasis is as important as the contrast between wish (faxint) and fact (faciunt). mea ⟨haec⟩ est. -- mala crux east quidem, Cas.416, "She's mine. -- She's a torment, that's what she is;" mea and mala crux are contrasted, and ea is emphasized. BA. sine, mea Pietas, te exorem. NI. exores tu me? SO. ego quidem ab hoc certe exorabo, Bac.1177; ego quidem obliquely contrasts the speaker with Bacchis, "(she may not) but I'll beseech this one," where hoc refers to another man, not Nicobulus. quasi fundum vendam, meis me addicam legibus. -- profundum vendis tu quidem, hau fundum, mihi, Capt.182; quidem both emphasizes tu and, despite attraction to the pronoun, opposes profundum to the preceding fundum. (Amphitruo, informed by his slave Sosia that there is another Sosia, has asked who he is) tuos est servos. -- mihi quidem uno te plus etiam est quam volo, Am.610; quidem objects to the thought of another Sosia ("but one of you is more than I want") and emphasizes the pronoun me, "for me (though perhaps not for someone else) one of you, etc." dormio, ne occlamites. -- tu quidem vigilas, Cur.184. quod faciam nil habeo miser. ille quidem hanc abducet, scio, Bac.634.

sed haec melius ex re et ex tempore constitues. mihi quidem usque curae erit quid agas, Cic.Fam.12.19.3; the contrast between "you" and "me" is quite weak. fluentes purpurissataeque buccae, dignae Capua, sed illa vetere; nam haec quidem quae nunc est splendidissimorum hominum . . . multitudine redundat, Pis.25; the clause with quidem is almost an afterthought. qui amicis L. Corneli aut inimici sunt aut invident, ii sunt huic multo vehementius pertimescendi. nam huic quidem ipsi quis est unquam inventus inimicus? Balb.58. qui de meis in vos meritis praedicaturus non sum, quae sunt adhuc et mea voluntate et vestra exspectatione leviora; sed tamen sui laboris milites semper eventu belli praemia petiverunt, qui qualis sit futurus ne vos quidem dubitatis. diligentiam quidem nostram aut, quem ad finem adhuc res processit, fortunam cur praeteream? Caes. Civ.2.32.11; the contrast between "your future rewards" and "my carefulness and good luck" is so weak that this Adversative-Emphatic quidem has almost become a particle of mere transition. (The speaker has been talking about Sulla's tyranny, though Sulla is not clearly the main subject) satellites quidem eius . . . nequeo satis mirari, Sal.Hist. 1.55.2, a vague contrast which marks almost nothing more than a change in focus.

fatalem rabiem temporis eius accusat cum velut contagione quadam pestifera non Ilergetes modo et Lacetani sed castra quoque Romana insanierint. suam quidem et fratris et reliquorum popularium eam condicionem esse ut . . ., Liv. 28.34.5; the speaker may have half-conceived a contrast between general circumstances affecting both Spaniards and Romans and considerations special to some of the Spaniards, but the contrast is so evanescent as to leave quidem mainly emphasizing suam, "and as for my own situation." credidere quidam testamento Alexandri distributas esse provincias, sed famam eius rei . . . vanam fuisse comperimus. et quidem suas, quas quisque opes divisis imperii partibus tuebantur, ipsi fundaverant, Curt.10.10.6 (text of Müller); the particle looks back to the preceding sentence, contrasting belief with fact, and insists on the truth of its own statement. alter multis volneribus confossus est, alter leviter quidem saucius, Sen.Ben.5.3.3, where leviter is emphasized by the suggested contrast with multis volneribus.

(we were saved by the doorkeeper) et Giton quidem iam dudum se ratione acutissima redemerat a cane, Petr.72.9; the contrast is weak, and quidem hardly does more than mark the change of subject, as also in the following sentence. praeterea habere in Africa trecenties sestertium fundis nominibusque depositum; nam familiam quidem tam magnam per agros Numidiae esse sparsam, ut possit vel Carthaginem capere, 117.8. (after speaking of the calamus Indicus) harundini quidem Indicae . . ., Plin.Nat.16.162. dicat fortasse aliquis, "non enim invehebatur." id quidem falso, Nat.36.5; quidem both emphasizes id and objects to the preceding statement. extemplo thalamis turbata paternis inferor. ille quidem dudum . . . agit versans secum, Stat.Theb.5.241; the opposition is feeble and quidem again serves mainly to call attention to the new subject.

hi sunt fere fines maxime inlustres et de quibus praecipue disputatur. nam omnis quidem persequi neque attinet neque possum, Quint.2.15.37; quidem glances back toward hi to effect a weak contrast between it and omnis. (Quintilian has been praising Homer for already displaying great ability in all aspects of rhetoric, illustration, inference, etc.) nam epilogus quidem quis umquam poterit illis Priami rogantis Achillem precibus aequari? 10.1.50; the peroration is loosely opposed to the other ingredients of a speech. (after talking of antonomasia for a paragraph) onomatopoeia quidem, 8.6.31. nec indignetur sibi Herodotus aequari Titum Livium, cum in narrando mirae iucunditatis clarissimique candoris, tum in contionibus supra quam enarrari potest eloquentem, ita quae dicuntur omnia cum rebus tum personis accomodata sunt: adfectus quidem . . . nemo historicorum commendavit magis, 10.1.101; one can feel an adversative force to quidem in the opposition between speeches and narration, on the one hand, and portrayal of emotion, on the other, and between being Herodotus' equal and being unsurpassed; but the opposition is weakly conceived, and quidem also singles out and emphasizes adfectus as the new focus of interest. (after talking about Macrinus' son) et de Macrino quidem, S.H.A.Op.Marc.4.1.

With equidem. ut vero conloqui cum Orpheo Musaeo Homero Hesiodo liceat, quanti tandem aestimatis? equidem saepe emori, si fieri posset, vellem, ut ea quae dico mihi liceret invisere, Cic.Tusc.1.98; the contrast between Cicero's opinion and that of his listeners is relatively unimportant.

Adversative-Limiting quidem. Limiting quidem also implies a reference to something else: "she (if no one else)," i.e. she at least. In practice this is very often indistinguishable from Emphatic (see below, p. 96), but a number of examples, mostly Ciceronian, are certain because the quidem phrase contains the word certe meaning "at any rate." Quidem opposes to the first idea a second which, in case the first is false, is true at a minimum. Quidem in these passages is in the middle between Adversative and Limiting. me consiliario fortasse non inperitissimo, fideli quidem et benevolo certe, Cic.Fam.1.9.2. quoniam, inquit, me una vobiscum servare non possum, vestrae quidem certe vitae prospiciam, Caes.Gal.7.50.4. spero tibi me causam probasse, cupio quidem certe, Cic.Att.1.1.4. si id minus, hoc quidem certe, Fam.6.3.2. huius domus est vel optima Messanae, notissima quidem certe et nostris hominibus apertissima maximeque hospitalis, Ver.4.3. bonae feminae, locupletis quidem certe, Phil.3.16, where Cicero is being sly; about Antony's wife he says, "a good woman, but (if not good, then) rich at least." habet populus Romanus ad quos gubernacula rei publicae deferat . . . habet quidem certe res publica adulescentis nobilissimos paratos defensores, Phil.2.113, "The people is at no loss whom to choose as rulers; . . . at any rate it certainly knows where to look for champions" (Mayor). Examples without certe: huic utinam aliquando gratiam referre possimus! habebimus quidem semper, Fam.14.14.2, "I hope someday we may be able to show our gratitude to him! At any rate we will always feel grateful." horum omnium (sc. cuniculorum) tria genera, si possis, in leporario habere oportet. duo quidem utique te habere puto, Var.R. 3.12.7, "You ought to have the three kinds. Two in any case I think you do have."

III. Emphatic *quidem*

The examples collected under this head are fewer than they might have been. In a sense all uses of *quidem* are emphatic. I have, however, when possible, attributed examples of *quidem* to other uses rather than to Emphatic, which I reserve for occasions when no direct contrast is expressed. So Emphatic *quidem* has been defined very narrowly. And by placing it here, after Contrasting and Adversative *quidem*, I may have suggested a false historical position for it. I suspect that *quidem* began as a merely emphatic particle; that in the earliest writings, mainly comedy, although examples of all its uses can be found, *quidem* is still inchoate (unless the colloquial material gives us a wrong impression); and that only afterwards, as Latin grows more precise, articulate, and settled, does it display a well-marked character. If I had been writing a historical account, I should then have begun with examples of Emphatic *quidem* where no contrast needs to be understood--there are very few such examples--followed them with examples where a contrast *is* intended, and only then gone on to describe the remaining range of *quidem*'s uses. But I am not confident that the material, being, as it is, most unevenly spread over time, genre, and stylistic level, will support such an account; and, further, *quidem* either possessed from the beginning or very soon acquired a certain lasting character, emphasis by contrast, which I aim to illuminate as clearly as possible. In the interests then of both honesty and usefulness I have curtailed the domain of Emphatic quidem and denied it first place. Contrasting quidem most clearly illustrates quidem's nature.

To repeat, I call Emphatic only those quidems where the contrast needs to be supplied by the reader. Dombart too perceives the connection between contrast and emphasis: "Die in 'quidem' liegende versichernde Kraft dient endlich auch dazu, einen Begriff besonders hervorzuheben und entspricht dann ganz der griechischen Partikel γέ. Auch dieses 'quidem' involvirt (wie γέ) einen Gegensatz, dessen erstes Glied aber meistens nicht ausgesprochen ist."[27] Even more useful is a comparison with the Greek particle μέν. Probably like quidem, μέν began as an emphatic particle, examples being found mainly in Homer and Pindar, and then developed into an antithetic particle. And, as with quidem, the connection is so close that the two uses, emphatic and contrasting, cannot always be distinguished. As Denniston says, p. 364: "It is often difficult to decide whether μέν is to be taken as purely emphatic or as suggesting an unexpressed antithesis (the so-called μέν solitarium);" or more pungently, p. 359: "It is often difficult to distinguish . . . μέν the bachelor from μέν the widower." An example

[27] Dombart (above, p. 10, n. 8), p. 209.

will make clear the correspondence of Emphatic <u>quidem</u> to μέν solitarium. apparet id quidem . . . etiam caeco, Liv. 32.34.2, is a translation of τοῦτο μὲν . . . καὶ τυφλῷ δῆλον, Polyb.18.4.3, where the μέν is certainly solitarium. The evidence of a similar Greek particle thus confirms the naturalness of <u>quidem</u>'s shift in meaning. In Greek, however, one use tended to drive out the other; in Latin the uses accumulated.

Emphatic <u>quidem</u> often cannot be distinguished from Limiting <u>quidem</u>. It is nearly impossible to decide whether <u>ut mihi quidem videtur</u> means "as it seems to <u>me</u> (though perhaps not everyone)" or "as it seems to me at least (though perhaps no one else)," and indeed only a tiny difference in degree separates these two translations. I have put in this section many examples which may well strike other readers as being Limiting, and have saved for that section only the very clearest cases.

Among the examples of Emphatic <u>quidem</u> we may discern different degrees in which the rest of the implied contrast is obvious. Sometimes the writer or speaker has some definite contrast in mind and the context makes it immediately obvious what that is. (after describing the different attitudes to their blindness of Tiresias and Polyphemus) recte hic quidem (i.e. Tiresias), Cic.<u>Tusc</u>.5.115; there is no formal contrast. (Cicero has been considering the roads he might take, e.g. the via Cassia and via Flaminia) restat Aurelia. hic quidem etiam praesidia habeo, Phil.12.23; hic quidem implies "here, as distinguished from on those other roads." non dicam miser--nam hoc quidem abhorret a virtute verbum--sed certe exercitus, Planc.78; hoc, referring to the word miser, is implicitly contrasted with what follows, exercitus. aut enim nemo, quod quidem magis credo, aut si quisquam, ille sapiens fuit, Amic.9; Seyffert explains: "das quidem beim Relativum dient zunächst, um durch die Restriction den Gegensatz zu schärfen: 'und dies ist mir das Wahrscheinlichere;'" as in the preceding example, only as the sentence unfolds does the writer indicate what other thing he had in mind. (Cicero has discussed and rejected money, honor, and beauty as goals for the sake of which virtue is desirable and now he mentions pleasure) in ea quidem (sc. voluptate) spernenda et repudianda virtus vel maxime cernitur, Leg.1.52. annis centenis quadragenis vivere . . . Aethiopas Macrobios et Seras existimat et qui Athon montem incolant, hos quidem quia viperinis carnibus alantur, Plin. Nat.7.27. (a house should not be too close to the shore) nec paludem quidem vicinam esse oportet aedificiis, Colum. 1.5.6, where "swamp" is emphasized by contrast with "shore." nec tam hoc praecipiendum est, ut quaestionem continens iudicationem inveniamus (nam id quidem facile est), quam ut intueamur semper, Quint.3.11.26. Examples of this sort are not far removed from those in which Adversative and Emphatic quidem are blended; see above, pp. 87-92.

Very often, however, the implicit contrast is more distant. mea quidem hercle certe in dubio vitast, Ter.An.347, where no one else's life is in question. illud quidem fatebitur Scaptius, Cic.Att.6.1.7; no other admission presents itself to the reader's mind. hos ergo asotos bene quidem vivere aut beate numquam dixerim, Fin.2.23, "I would not say they live well," implying, for instance, "though perhaps they live comfortably." ista quidem quia nota mihi tua, magne, voluntas, Iuppiter, et Turnum et terras invita reliqui, Verg.A.12.808, where Juno is not feigning ignorance of any other of Jupiter's intentions.

In most of the examples quoted, quidem follows and emphasizes a pronoun, either demonstrative or personal or relative. But, as we have seen in the other uses also, Emphatic quidem, though attracted to pronouns, does not always emphasize them. In these cases quidem frequently acts as a sentence adverb, insisting on the truth of the whole statement; we may translate it "really, indeed, truly." This force of the particle can often be felt in other uses as well. inscita ecastor tu quidem es, Plaut.Mos.208. It seems clear from the context that tu is not really the stressed word; the sense is not so much "boy, you are dumb" as "boy, you really are dumb," Notice how in English we have a different way of emphasizing the sentence as a whole: we put weight on the verb, either by a stress in speech

(represented by italics, "she _likes_ me") or with an auxilia-
ry verb ("she does like me"); Latin prefers to strengthen a
pronoun, usually the subject.

I submit some examples where I think _quidem_ does not
actually emphasize the pronoun. edepol haec quidem bellu-
last, Plaut.<u>Mil</u>.988, "she's really a doll." edictiones ae-
dilicas hicquidem habet, <u>Capt</u>.823, "this guy's acting like
an <u>aedile</u>." puer est ille quidem, stulta, <u>Mer</u>.540, "he's
just a <u>boy</u>, you dope." iam ista quidem apsumpta res erit,
<u>Mos</u>.235, "his property will surely be squandered soon;" the
MSS. have <u>quidem</u> <u>absumpta</u> <u>quidem</u>, and <u>absumpta</u> <u>quidem</u> is
adopted by some editors, which would be like the English em-
phasis. hicquidem pol summam in crucem cena aut prandio
perduci potest, <u>St</u>.625. puer quidem beatust, <u>Truc</u>.808, "the
kid sure is lucky," where <u>quidem</u> is displaced, but not next
to a pronoun. sed quis hic est qui huc pergit? attat,
hi(c)quidem est parasitus Gnatho militis, Ter.<u>Eu</u>.228. certe
Eurypylus hic quidem est, Enn.<u>scen</u>.166. pater igitur amens,
qui odisset eum sine causa quem procrearat? at is quidem
fuit omnium constantissimus, Cic.<u>S</u>.<u>Rosc</u>.41. dum genus hominum, dum populi Romani nomen exstabit--quod quidem erit,
si per te licebit, sempiternum, <u>Phil</u>.2.51, "which <u>will</u> be
eternal, if you let it." istud quidem, inquit, faciam, Nep.
<u>Ep</u>.4.4, "I <u>will</u> indeed do that." et hic quidem morbus celer-
iter in Italia restinctus est, Plin.<u>Nat</u>.26.8. This example
is less certain: audite . . . ea quae saepissime inter me

et Scipionem de amicitia disserebantur. quamquam ille quidem nihil difficilius esse dicebat quam amicitiam usque ad
extremum vitae diem permanere, Cic.Amic.33; quidem might emphasize ille ("he" as opposed to "I") or the whole clause
("though he did use to say"). With equidem. equidem fabulam et fictam rem ducebam, Liv.34.2.3; the context makes it
clear that he means "I used to think so (but I don't any
more)."

Examples of Emphatic quidem. patrem huc orato ut veni-
at. -- iam dudum est intus. -- hac quidem non venit, Plaut.
As.741, "He didn't come this way (and so he must have en-
tered the house some other way);" the next line is: angi-
porto illac per hortum circum iit clam. nunc quidem praeter
nos nemo est. dic mihi verum serio, Am.855; as Dombart
says,[28] the quidem implies a contrast which is not expressed: "As long as your husband was present, you might
have had some reason for concealing the truth." anne opor-
tuit? -- ita te quidem, qui es familiaris, Truc.667, "Is it
necessary? -- It is for you." nam ubi mores deteriores in-
crebrescunt in dies, ubique amici qui infideles sient neque-
as pernoscere, ubique id eripiatur animo tuo quod placeat
maxume, ibi quidem si regnum detur, non cupitast civitas,
Mer.841. nimi' stulte faciunt mea quidem sententia, Men.81.

[28]Dombart (above, p. 10, n. 8), p. 209.

meum quidem te lectum certe occupare non sinam, Truc.963.
mihi quidem tu iam eras mortuos, Per.20. iam huc adveniet
miles. -- et miles quidem? Bac.222. mille nummum poscit.
-- et poscit quidem? Ter.Hau.606. The Oxford Latin Dictionary, s.v. "et" 15b, classifies these two phrases as sarcas-
tic and translates them "a soldier is he?" and "so he's de-
manding, is he?" dic sodes, pater, tibi vero quid istic est
rei? -- nil mi quidem, Ter.Ad.644.

(after discussing different kinds of land and what they
are suitable for) Stolo "Cato quidem" inquit "gradatim prae-
ponens . . .," Var.R.1.7.9, where Cato's opinion is not contrasted with that of any one in particular. eam gloriam
quam nemo meo quidem iudicio est postea consecutus, Cic.
Brut.32. habet autem ut in aetatibus auctoritatem senectus,
sic in exemplis antiquitas, quae quidem apud me ipsum valet
plurimum, Orat.169, "and this is the thing that holds the
greatest importance for me." mihi quidem ipsi nihil ab istis iam noceri potest, Catil.3.27. utinam quidem haec ipsa
non modo iniquorum invidiae sed aequorum exspectationi satis
facere posset!, Sul.54; the implied contrast is sed non
potest; cf. the examples of utinam quidem under Contrasting
quidem solum (above, pp. 72-73). ut mihi quidem videtur,
Sen.76. hosne igitur laudas et hanc eorum, inquam, sententiam sequi nos censes oportere? minime vero istorum quidem,
inquit, Fin.3.12, "no, certainly not their opinion." quod
quidem si acciderit, omnia nobis erunt meliora, Att.16.3.4,

"if this shall come about, all will be better for us."

quae quidem res Caesari non minorem quam ipsa victoria voluptatem attulit, Caes.Gal.1.53.6; there is an implied contrast with ipsa victoria. nam me quidem ex animi mei sententia nulla oratio laedere potest, Sal.Jug.85.27. quae quidem res mihi in primis videtur causa fuisse facinus maturandi, Cat.15.3, "that seems to me the principal cause." carpit enim viris paulatim uritque videndo femina, nec nemorum patitur meminisse nec herbae dulcibus illa quidem inlecebris, et saepe superbos cornibus inter se subigit decernere amantis, Verg.G.3.217; illa quidem is almost like an interjected reminder, "she's the one, mind you." iste quidem veteres inter ponetur honeste, qui vel mense brevi vel toto est iunior anno, Hor.Ep.2.1.43. ista quidem sententia, inquit, ea est, quae neque amicos parat nec inimicos tollit, Liv.9.3.12.

craticii vero (sc. parietes) velim quidem ne inventi essent, Vitr.2.8.20, "I might wish so," implying "but they have been invented;" compare the next two quotations. sed satin omnia ex sententia? -- vellem quidem, Ter.Ph.257; one can supply after vellem quidem something like sed ita non est; the implication that all is not as desired does not escape the first speaker, who now says: quid istuc est?, "what's the matter?" utinam quidem sufficeret largior scaena, Petr.117.2; we understand sed vero non sufficit. (after a digression on the temple of Ammon and its oracle) ac tum quidem regem propius adeuntem maximus natu e sacerdotibus filium appellat, Curt.4.7.25; the emphasis on _tum_ serves to recall us to the point in the narrative where we left off. illi quidem (sc. vetusti) non aurum nec argentum nec perlucidos ⟨lapides in⟩ ima terrarum faece quaerebant, Sen.Ep. 90.45, "they did not (but we do)." "non negabis" inquit "te (sc. beneficium) recepisse." et cum respondisset "quando?" "saepe quidem" inquit "et multis locis," Ben.2.11.2. nam id quidem maxime contrarium est, Colum.4.11.3. ne quid sciens quidem praeteream, Plin.Nat.17.137, implying the possibility that he may omit something unwittingly. sit mens ista quidem cunctis, ut vestra recusent fata, Luc.3.324; the implied contrast may be "but I doubt that it is so," in which case _quidem_ goes with the whole clause, not just _ista_. de omnibus rebus oratori dicendum arbitratur his quidem verbis, Quint.2.21.5, "in precisely these words (and no others)." miserat etiam epistulas . . . iactantes et gloriosas, his quidem verbis: "Io io, liber ad te venio," Plin.Ep.3.9.13. iste quidem Argolicis haud olim indebitus armis luctus adest, Stat.Theb.5.735. et Maternus, mihi quidem, inquit, susceptum a te munus adeo peregisse nondum videris, ut . . ., Tac.Dial.33.1. eumque muneratus est, ita ut privatus pro loco suo posset honeste vivere, his quidem muneribus: agris, bubus, equis, frumento, etc., S.H.A.Sev.Alex.32.3. quas quidem tabulas post mortem eius senatus et deponi iussit et exuri, Max.12.11, "these were the tablets."

Examples of Emphatic equidem. equidem pol vel falso tamen laudari multo malo quam vero culpari, Plaut.Mos.178. equidem Sosia Amphitruoni' sum, Am.411. facile equidem facere possum si iubes, Ter.Hau.547. sanum te credis esse? -- equidem arbitror, Ad.748, "Do you believe you're well? -- Yes, I do think so." equidem non dubito quin . . ., Var. L.9.32. non equidem dubito, Catul.108.3, the only instance in Catullus. equidem fateor, Sal.Hist.2.98.4. certe equidem audieram, Verg.Ecl.9.7; the speaker is aware that what he has heard may not be true, "I did hear it (but it may be wrong);" his companion in fact makes explicit his implied doubts: audieras et fama fuit; sed carmina tantum nostra valent . . . haud equidem tali me dignor honore, A.1.335. dicam equidem, licet arma mihi mortemque minetur, A.11.348; not ego, but the whole clause is emphasized, "I shall say so." numquid de Dacis audisti? -- nil equidem, Hor.S.2.6. 53. equidem nec quid taceam nec quatenus proloquar invenio, Liv.39.15.4. non equidem miror, si stat victoria tecum, Ov. Ep.10.105. sacrum quoque, quod equidem dis minime cordi esse crediderim, Curt.4.3.23. itaque hoc tibi philosophia praestabit, quo equidem nihil maius existimo, Sen.Ep.115.18. quin immo etiam exstant commentarii auctorum--quos non equidem demonstrabo, Plin.Nat.37.197. equidem haec ad quaedam prodesse non negaverim, Quint.11.2.23. equidem saepe in agmine . . . fortissimi cuiusque voces audiebam, Tac.Agr.33.4, "I myself, in my own person, have heard." beatissimus equidem sum, Fro.Ant.1.p.302 (105N).

One idiom deserves to be singled out: hoc quidem . . . est, non . . . Here too quidem is attracted to the pronoun. hoc quidem "profecto" certum est, non est arbitrarium, Plaut. Am.372. nam hoc quidem pol e robigine, non est e ferro factum, Rud.1300. id quidem optundere auditorem est, non rem expolire, Rhet.Her.4.54. optare hoc quidem est, non disputare, Cic.Fat.46. optare hoc quidem est, non docere, Tusc. 2.30. praecipitare istuc quidem est, non descendere, N.D. 1.89. decipere hoc quidem est, non iudicare, Off.1.33. Holden in explaining the last passage suggests the essentially contrastive nature of Emphatic quidem: "quidem gives emphasis to the pronoun and is equivalent to si quid aliud, profecto, 'this, if anything else,' 'this surely.'"

In several sentences Cicero did not quite carry out his original intention, I suspect; the changing turn of thought obscures the second half of a contrast. We may consider the resulting quidems as Contrasting quidems manqués and so a species of Emphatic. (Cicero had digressed to talk about body and soul) et summatim quidem haec erant de corpore animoque dicenda, quibus quasi informatum est quid hominis natura postulat. ex quo perspicuum est . . ., Fin.5.37; the implied contrast is something like sed amplius nunc licet de hominis natura disserere. (after describing Romulus' choosing and fortifying a site for his city) atque haec quidem perceleriter confecit; nam et urbem constituit . . . et ad firmandam novam civitatem novum quoddam et subagreste consilium . . . secutus est, Rep.2.12; the sentence begins as if it were going to continue alia maiora instabant: urbs constituenda, etc., but instead we get a statement of what Romulus did next. ac de hac quidem divina atque immortali laude Bruti (sc. regni sublati) silebo . . . tantamne patientiam, di boni! tantam moderationem, tantam in iniuria tranquillitatem et modestiam! Phil.10.7; Stamm correctly explains: "Man hat zu denken: 'de hac quidem laude (regni sublati) silebo; sed videte quae aliae virtutes in eo fuerint.'"[29]

In all the above examples some contrast, near or distant, was implied with the word emphasized by quidem. Occasionally quidem emphasizes without any contrast. We might say that in these cases quidem strengthens the preceding word; it very closely approaches γέ. nempe ergo aperte vis quae restat me loqui? -- sane quidem, Ter.An.195, "yes, indeed." optumam quidem mulierem, Ad.974. populi Romani igitur est patronus L. Antonius? malam quidem illi pestem! Cic.Phil.6.12. proinde desinant quidam quaerere ultra aut opinari, mihique, qui compertum habeo, credant; aut quidem vetustissima nave impositos quocumque vento in quascumque

---

[29] Peter Stamm, "Die Partikelverbindung 'et quidem' ('ac quidem') bei Cicero," Progr. Rössel (1885), p. 7.

terras iubebo avehi, Caes.<u>orat</u>.42; <u>quidem</u> emphasizes the disjunction, as also at Plaut.<u>Mos</u>.944, Ter.<u>Ph</u>.425, and Cic. <u>Att</u>.16.11.6 (the other examples listed in <u>Thes</u>. <u>Ling</u>. <u>Lat</u>., 2.1573 are wrong). at dixi fluere hunc lutulentum, saepe ferentem plura quidem tollenda relinquendis, Hor.<u>S</u>.1.10.51. certa quidem tantis causa et manifesta ruinis, Prop.3.13.3. libenter quidem parui ancillae, Petr.129.12. grande quidem rarumque viris, Stat.<u>Silv</u>.1.2.106. per omnes quidem species rerum cotidie paene nascentium, Quint.2.5.14. defenderam reos ingenti quidem coetu, Plin.<u>Ep</u>.7.6.9.

Finally let us look at a pair of passages where the force of <u>quidem</u> is particularly inchoate and diffuse. I call these <u>quidem</u>s Emphatic because they lack clear direction. essurire mihi videre. -- miquidem essurio, non tibi, Plaut.<u>Capt</u>.866; this might be merely Emphatic, or Adversative (correcting the first speaker's <u>mihi</u>), or (with <u>non tibi</u>) Contrasting <u>quidem</u> <u>solum</u>. atque mea quidem ⟨eadem⟩ sententia est, Cic.<u>Leg</u>.2.24; either Extending ("and, what is more, I think so too," i.e. I add my opinion to yours), or Emphatic ("<u>I</u> think so too"), or Limiting ("I at least think so too").

IV. Limiting *quidem*

As indicated above, p. 96, Limiting is often difficult to distinguish from Emphatic *quidem*, and not a few of the examples quoted there might belong here. I merely cite now several passages where the Limiting force seems relatively clear. non me quidem faciet auctore hodie ut illum decipiat, Plaut.St.602, "I at least won't be responsible for his deceiving him." oratio autem vel optima esset illo quidem tempore orationum omnium, Cic.Brut.100. vellem . . . ne deteruissent alios a studiis. quamquam te quidem video minime esse deterritum, Fin.1.26, where Adversative *quidem* is also possible. huic alii parem esse dicebant, alii anteponebant L. Crassum. illud quidem certe omnes ita iudicabant, neminem esse qui horum altero utro patrono cuiusquam ingenium requireret, Brut.143; this example too might be called mildly Adversative. sed tamen quicquid erit in his libellis, quantulumcumque videbitur esse, hoc quidem certe manifestum erit, Ver.2.183. quod nos quidem iucundissimum arbitramur, Nep.Att.14.1. quantum quidem ego sciam, Sen.Dial.6.4.3, "at least so far as I know." With *equidem*. quantum equidem intellego, Cic.Fin.4.13. ut equidem arbitror, Plin.Nat.35.10.

If it were only a matter of such examples we would be entitled even to doubt the Limiting force of *quidem*. Examples found in relative clauses, however, seem indisputable; see Kühner-Stegmann, 2.307-08. ac nostrae fere causae, quae quidem sunt criminum, plerumque infitiatione defenduntur, Cic.de Orat.2.105. cum in suo quemque opere artificem, qui quidem excellat, nihil aliud cogitare meditari curare videam, nisi quo sit in illo genere melior, Rep.1.35. Peripateticorum omnium, quos quidem ego audierim, meo iudicio facile princeps, Tim.2. nec vero habeo quemquam antiquiorem, cuius quidem scripta proferenda putem, Brut.61. ut unus post hominum memoriam, quem quidem nos audierimus, cognomine Iustus sit appellatus, Nep.Ar.1.2. prima Romanis inita provinciarum, quae quidem continentis sint, Liv.28.12.12. ergo natura permixta est omnibus istis ratio, quae quidem oratio est vere, Quint.12.2.20. This last example is interesting: non vinum ⟨viris⟩ moderari, sed viri vino solent, qui quidem probi sunt; verum qui inprobust si quasi bibit sive adeo caret temeto, tamen ab ingenio inprobust, Plaut.Truc.832; the quidem starts out as Limiting, "at least those who are upright," but then becomes Contrasting as the speaker turns to those who are wicked.

V. Extending quidem

Extending quidem resembles in form Adversative: both look back to the previous statement. But whereas Adversative quidem opposes, weakens, or detracts from the preceding, Extending quidem prolongs or adds to it. That these two cannot always be distinguished is to be expected.

In the most transparent examples the phrase with quidem repeats a word from the previous phrase and makes some addition to it. In these short examples et quidem is found as a rule; but all et quidems need not be Extending, nor do all Extending quidems require et. In the longer examples quidem most often appears alone. emissus aliquis e carcere. et quidem emissus per imprudentiam, Cic.Planc.31, "let out from jail, and, what is more, let out through imprudence." dixit, et bis quidem dixit, Clu.103. volui interdiu eum post lustrationem, cum concurrimus, et quidem, si diis placet, lustrationum die occidere, Liv.40.13.2, "after the lustration, and indeed on the very day of the lustrations." cupit regnum, et quidem scelerate cupit, Liv.40.11.7. nec domum esse hoc corpus sed hospitium, et quidem breve hospitium, Sen.Ep.120.14. venit in nostras manus tandem Thyestes, venit et totus quidem, Sen.Thy.495. tum se quieti dedit et quievit verissimo quidem somno, Plin.Ep.6.16.13. est igitur in pedibus, et metricis quidem pedibus, Quint.9.4.52.

Scarcely different are the examples in which a repeated

word is easily supplied by the reader. tantum doleo, ac mirifice quidem, Cic.Att.2.19.1, where doleo is understood with mirifice again. proinde istuc facias ipse quod faciamus nobis suades. -- ego vero, et quidem edepol lubens, Plaut.As.645. tune huic credis? -- plus quidem quam tibi aut--mihi, Capt.572. duo milia iugerum campi Leontini Sex. Clodio rhetori adsignasti et quidem immunia, Cic.Phil.2.43. accipe quotiens id fecerint, et quidem semper bono publico, Liv.34.5.8. nox est et quidem horrida ac terribilis, Sen. Nat.3.27.10. positus erat primae magnitudinis aper, et quidem pilleatus, Petr.40.3. ita nec praeceptor deerat, optimus quidem et electissimus, qui faciem eloquentiae, non imaginem praestaret, Tac.Dial.34.5. non enim preces sunt istud, sed efflagitatio, intempestiva quidem et improvisa, Ann.2.38. decessit Corellius Rufus et quidem sponte, Plin. Ep.1.12.1. ego, ille quem nosti, apros tres et quidem pulcherrimos cepi, Ep.1.6.1. dato igitur stipendio, et quidem ingenti, S.H.A.Max.18.4. With equidem. sit modus; et fore credo equidem, Val.Flac.4.476. crede, inquis, mihi. credo equidem, sed scio quam cupias minui dolorem meum, Cic.Att. 11.6.2; the equidem accompanies the repeated credo and also introduces the first half of a contrast, i.e. it is both Extending and Contrasting.

In exchange of speakers. As in the example directly preceding and the one from Plautus' Captivi, Extending quidem is often used in an exchange of speakers, when the second agrees with the first and adds something of his own. Naturally, most examples are found in comedy. eo ego hinc hau longe. -- et quidem ego ⟨eo⟩ hau longe, Plaut.Per.217. tun me vidisti? -- atque his quidem hercle oculis, Mil.368. at pol nitent (sc. oves), hau sordidae videntur ambae. -- attonsae hae quidem ambae usque sunt, Bac.1125. amat mulier quaedam quendam. -- pol istuc quidem multae, Mil. 1017. In the last three instances note that quidem is attracted to a pronoun. vos date bibat tibicini. -- et quidem nobis, St.758. e caelo? -- atque medio quidem, Trin.941. abeo. -- et quidem ego ibo domum, Mil.259. quin abeo? -- et quidem ego? Ter.Ph.209. sed quid mi obtigerit scio. -- et quidem ego, An.967. vae misero mihi. -- et mihi quidem, Hec.606. sic plane iudico. -- et rectissime quidem iudicas, Cic.Rep.3.44. et vero ita existimo. -- humanum id quidem, quod ita existumas, Tusc.3.12. With equidem. i in malam rem! -- ibi sum equidem, Plaut.Poen.295. sine. -- sino equidem, si lubet, Bac.99. sed perge cetera. -- pergam equidem, Cic.Leg.2.69.

Larger examples. We now turn to some examples in which the whole idea of the previous clause is being extended, and the quidem cannot be said to look back to any one word. optumam quidem mulierem. -- et quidem tuo nepoti hui(u)s filio hodie prima mammam dedit haec, Ter.Ad.974, the first quidem being Emphatic, "A very good woman indeed. -- Yes, and,

what's more, she was the first to suckle your grandson."
sese ipse dicit . . . hanc cupere uxorem. -- modone quae inventast? -- eam: et quidem iubebit posci, Hau.775, "she's the one (he wants as his wife), and, moreover, he's going to have them ask for her in marriage." in confirmandis autem nostris argumentationibus infirmandisque contrariis saepe erunt accusatori motus animorum incitandi, reo mitigandi. atque hoc quidem utrique maxime in peroratione faciendum, Cic.Part.122, "and, furthermore, each one must especially do this in his peroration." itaque imbuendus est is, qui iocose volet dicere, quasi natura quadam apta ad haec genera et moribus, ut ad cuiusque modi genus ridiculi vultum etiam accomodetur; qui quidem quo severior est et tristior . . . hoc illa, quae dicuntur, salsiora videri solent, de Orat.2.289. tradamus nos ei (sc. philosophiae) curandos: sanabimur, si volemus. et progrediar quidem longius: non enim de aegritudine solum . . . sed de omni animi, ut ego posui, perturbatione, morbo, ut Graeci volunt, explicabo, Tusc.3.13. dialecticorum vero verba nulla sunt publica, suis utuntur. et id quidem commune omnium fere est artium; aut enim nova sunt rerum novarum facienda nomina aut ex aliis transferenda, Acad.1.25; quidem extends a particular case to a general rule. Philippum et Nabim, hostes et bello superatos ab T. Quinctio, tamen in regno relictos. Philippo quidem anno priore etiam stipendium remissum et filium obsidem redditum, Liv.37.25.12, "Philip and Nabis were left on the throne; and

Philip, moreover, had his tribute remitted and his son returned;" Weissenborn-Müller describe this as "<u>quidem</u> steigernd." itaque eligendum est, a quo beneficium accipiam; et quidem diligentius quaerendus beneficii quam pecuniae creditor, Sen.<u>Ben</u>.2.18.5. adeo illa ipsa, quae dura et adversa dicturo videbantur, secunda dicenti fuerunt. Caesar quidem tantum mihi studium, tantam etiam curam . . . praestitit, ut . . ., Plin.<u>Ep</u>.2.11.15.

With <u>equidem</u>. insanum bonam (sc. domum). non equidem ullam in publico maiorem hac existumo, Plaut.<u>Mos</u>.909, "a great house--and what's more, I don't think there's a better one around." Priamus . . . non quinquaginta modo, quadringentos filios habet atque equidem omnis lectos sine probro, <u>Bac</u>.974; all MSS. have <u>equidem</u>, but editors regularly emend to <u>quidem</u>, "fortasse recte," as Lindsay says. maximo cuique id accidere animo certum habeo ut se non cum praesentibus modo sed cum omnis aevi claris viris comparent. equidem haud dissimulo me tuas, Q. Fabi, laudes non adsequi solum velle sed . . . etiam exsuperare, Liv.28.43.7; perhaps there is also a slight contrast between all great men and the speaker.

Examples of Extending <u>quidem</u>. sed ita adsimulatote quasi ego sim peregrinus. -- scilicet, et quidem quasi tu nobiscum adveniens hodie oraveris . . ., Plaut.<u>Poen</u>.601. ita fiunt omnium partes minimum octoginta et una, et quidem necessariae nec parvae, Var.R.2.1.13. is L. Crasso Q. Scaevola consulibus primum in foro dixit et apud hos quidem consules, Cic.Brut.229, "not only in the year of their consulship, but in their very presence." sed vobis voluptatum perceptarum recordatio vitam beatam facit, et quidem corpore perceptarum, Fin.2.106. vivere arbitror et eam quidem vitam quae est sola vita nominanda, Sen.77. at erat mecum senatus, et quidem veste mutata, Planc.87. conscende nobiscum, et quidem ad puppim, Fam.12.25.5. animadvertebas igitur, etsi tum nemo erat admodum copiosus, verum tamen versus ab is admisceri orationi. -- ac multos quidem a Dionysio Stoico, Tusc.2.26; the first speaker had said that the philosophers mixed verses into their discourse, and the second, agreeing, adds that Dionysius mixed in many verses. non enim audivit ille draconem loquentem sed est visus audire, et quidem, quo maius sit, cum radicem ore teneret locutus est, Div.2.141. beata vita glorianda et praedicanda et prae se ferenda est. . . . et quidem, nisi ea vita beata est, quae est eadem honesta, sit aliud necesse est melius vita beata, Tusc.5.50; Dougan in effect defines the range of Extending quidem when he explains: "'and furthermore,' introducing a new argument, an extension of the more frequent use in which it amplifies a preceding statement by the addition of a word or clause;" here the quidem might also be Adversative.

hunc infamatum a plerisque tres gravissimi historici

summis laudibus extulerunt: Thucydides . . . Theopompus . . . et Timaeus; qui quidem duo maledicentissimi nescio quo modo in illo uno laudando consenserunt, Nep.Alc.11.1, "and, what is more, the latter two, though most scurrilous, agree only in their praise of this man." hanc boni beatique omnes amatis, et quidem, quod indignum est, omnes pusilli et semitarii moechi, Catul.37.15, the only quidem in Catullus. nec id mirari debent aut possunt, cum Italiae urbes, Regium Tarentum Capuam . . . eidem subiectas videant imperio. Capua quidem sepulcrum ac monumentum Campani populi . . . superest, Liv.31.29.11. qui tamen plura verba in castigandis matronis quam in rogatione nostra dissuadenda consumpsit, et quidem ut in dubio poneret utrum id quod reprenderet matronae sua sponte an nobis auctoribus fecissent, Liv.34.5.3, "and, what is more, with the result that he left it in doubt whether . . ." sed qui diligentius perquisierunt, tradiderunt eos (sc. ventos) esse octo, maxime quidem Andronicus Cyrrestes, Vitr.1.6.4. cubiculum regis solus intravi, ferro quidem cinctus, Curt.6.10.21.

adsentior, eo quidem magis, quod scio . . ., Sen.Dial. 1.5.6. ego vero hoc ipsum solacii loco pono, et quidem valentissimi, Nat.6.2.1. Clitum carissimum sibi et una educatum inter epulas transfodit manu quidem sua, Dial.5.17.1, "he killed his dear friend, and, moreover, by his own hand." et nos sequemur in vitibus hanc ipsam rationem, tanto quidem magis quod . . ., Colum.3.10.18. supervenere alieni et quidem externi, ut Numa Romulo successerit ex Sabinis veniens, Inscr. Dessau 212. Livia Rutili LXXXXVII annos excessit . . . Clodia Ofili CXV, haec quidem etiam enixa quindeciens, Plin.Nat.7.158. cocleae prosunt et cum testis suis tusae; cum murra quidem et ture etiam praecisos nervos sanare dicuntur, Nat.30.116. flagrat . . . mons Chimaera et quidem immortali diebus ac noctibus flamma, Nat.2.236. boves animalium soli et retro ambulantes pascuntur, apud Garamantas quidem haut aliter, Nat.8.178.

Servium quidem Galbam miseratione sola . . . elapsum esse . . . testatum est, Quint.2.15.8; the previous example had made the weaker point that extra-rhetorical means could be useful, whereas Servius Galba is proof that sometimes such means are indispensable. eaedem poenae in Laelium Balbum decernuntur, id quidem a laetantibus, quia Balbus truci eloquentia habebatur, promptus adversum insontes, Tac.Ann. 6.48. uxore ab Octavia, nobili quidem et probitatis spectatae, . . . abhorrebat, Ann.13.12, "not only was she his wife but, moreover, a distinguished and virtuous woman." ceterum per omnem valetudinem eius crebrius quam ex more principatus per nuntios visentis et libertorum primi et medicorum intimi venere, sive cura illud sive inquisitio erat. supremo quidem die momenta ipsa deficientis per dispositos cursores nuntiata constabat, nullo credente sic adcelerari quae tristis audiret, Agr.43.3. gratias egi libentissime quidem, Plin.Ep.7.7.1. cunctos et armatos, et quidem ardentissimo ingenio, Ep.7.25.6. confecerunt me infirmitates meorum, mortes etiam, et quidem iuvenum, Ep.8.16.1. Antonius, despiciens etiam maternam Augusti originem, proavam eius Afri generis fuisse et modo unguentariam tabernam, modo pistrinum Ariciae exercuisse obicit. Cassius quidem Parmensis quadam epistula non tantum ut pistoris, sed etiam ut nummulari nepotem sic taxat Augustum, Suet.Aug.4.2. capite punire et quidem ante principia se coram, Suet.Otho 1.2. lignum a me toto oppido et quidem oppido quaesitum, Apul.Apol.62. nos tamen ex diversis historicis eruta in lucem proferemus, et ea quidem quae memoratu digna erunt, S.H.A.Op.Macr.1.1. circumstantibus etiam militibus et quidem armatis, Sev.Alex. 53.4.

Adversative-Extending quidem. Not rarely Extending and Adversative quidem come so close to one another that they cannot be distinguished; quidem looks backwards, but we cannot tell whether it suggests a contrast more than a continuation. Examples of this borderline state were given above under Adversative quidem, pp. 85-87; here I add a few problematic ones.

longiore certamine sensim residere Samnitium animos, Gallorum quidem etiam corpora intolerantissima laboris atque aestus fluere, Liv.10.28.4. One would be in real difficulty if forced to decide on this passage: the contrast between "the spirits of the Samnites" and "the bodily strength of

the Gauls" inclines one to Adversative; but the strong etiam
and the difference in degree between "gradually sink" and
"flow away" urge Extending. odisti me, non quidem provoca-
tus; sed finge iustum intulisse te bellum: cum feminis ergo
agere debueras?, Curt.4.10.29, either "you hate me, though
without provocation" or "you hate me and, moreover, you do
so without provocation;" in either case the quidem becomes
Contrasting with the following clause. bonum virum facile
crederes, magnum libenter. et ipse quidem, quamquam medio
in spatio integrae aetatis ereptus, quantum ad gloriam,
longissimum aevum peregit, Tac.Agr.44.3. This is a very
difficult passage, which I place here hesitatingly. Quidem
may point to the contrast between what you might have thought
and what he himself actually was (hence, Adversative) or emphasize the superiority of fact to opinion, as if to say
"not only in your opinion, but, what is more, in actual
fact" (Extending). The choice, if it needs to be made, is
rendered more perilous by uncertainty whether goodness and
greatness are synonymous with glory, which favors the case
of Extending quidem, or are distinct from it, which favors
Adversative. One might even argue that quidem is also Emphatic, pressing ipse and the truth of the whole sentence.
But such unresolvable ambiguities inhere in a particle like
quidem.

VI. Alleged use of quidem to introduce examples

Many have claimed that quidem is used in introducing examples. Grossmann, pp. 51-52, gives the most instances, while Ludewig, pp. 28-29, Kühner ad Cic.Tusc.1.116, Gudeman ad Tac.Dial.11.2, and Kühner-Stegmann, 1.803, among others, also contribute to the argument. This, I believe, is a mistake, though an understandable one: quidem never does serve the purpose of introducing an example, but certain usages will naturally occur with examples. In part these scholars have been led to their conclusion under the bewitchment of the form, here a proper noun followed by quidem. The passages adduced to support the theory, nearly all drawn from Cicero or his imitator Quintilian, on closer inspection will be seen to fall within the range of quidem's uses as already described. All of the passages discussed are cited by one or more of the authors named above.

Some of the passages adduced are really Adversative. si voluptas summum sit bonum, affirmatis nullam omnino (sc. amicitiam) fore. de qua Epicurus quidem ita dicit, omnium rerum, quas ad beate vivendum sapientia comparaverit, nihil esse maius amicitia, nihil uberius, nihil iucundius, Cic. Fin.1.65, "and yet Epicurus . . .;" far from being an example, Epicurus is a counter-example, and his exaltation of friendship is contrasted with the others' denial of its very existence. cui (sc. Theodoro philosopho) cum Lysimachus rex crucem minaretur, istis, quaeso, inquit, ista horribilia minitare purpuratis tuis: Theodori quidem nihil interest, humine an sublime putescat, Tusc.1.102. (after examples of Demosthenes' sagacity drawn from several speeches) Ciceronis quidem vel una pro Cluentio quamlibet multis exemplis sufficiet oratio, Quint.6.5.9; Cicero is contrasted with Demosthenes, balanced rather than opposed.

Many of the alleged passages turn out to be Extending quidems: the reader is offered not so much an example as a new, further point. virorum fortium memoriam honore deorum inmortalium consecratam. ob eam enim ipsam causam Erectheus Athenis filiaeque eius in numero deorum sunt, itemque est delubrum Athenis quod Leocorion nominatur. Alabandenses quidem sanctius Alabandum colunt, a quo est urbs illa condita, quam quemquam nobilium deorum, Cic.N.D.3.50; an eponymous hero worshipped with greater reverence than a god is obviously a stronger case than a hero worshipped as a god. est autem etiam vehementer utile iis, qui honeste posse multum volunt, per hospites apud externos populos valere opibus et gratia. Theophrastus quidem scribit Cimonem Athenis etiam in suos curialis Laciadas hospitalem fuisse, Off.2.64; Reid, who glosses quidem here as "for instance," nevertheless paraphrases the thought "he was liberal (not only to strangers, but) even to members of his own ward." etsi ipsa ista defectio virium adulescentiae vitiis efficitur saepius quam senectutis; libidinosa enim et intemperans adulescentia effetum corpus tradit senectuti. Cyrus quidem apud Xenophontem . . . negat se umquam sensisse senectutem suam imbecilliorem factam quam adulescentia fuisset, Sen.30; Cyrus' statement that old age was no weaker than youth is an extension of Cicero's, who said only that the infirmities of old age are due to the vices of youth. si enim quod numquam vidimus, id quale sit intellegere non possumus, certe et deum ipsum et divinum animum corpore liberatum cogitatione complecti possumus. Dichaearchus quidem et Aristoxenus, quia difficilis erat animi quid aut qualis esset intellegentia, nullum omnino animum esse dixerunt, Tusc.1.51. This is probably an extension of the si clause, "we cannot perhaps understand the nature of something invisible; they went so far as to disbelieve in its existence;" this is also the view of Seyffert (ad Amic.24), who glosses quidem as atque adeo. Or the quidem may be Adversative, opposing their skepticism to the speaker's assertion that we can understand the soul. In any case, this quidem, cited by four writers as introducing an example, does nothing of the sort. (nothing more insane than anger) quid Achille Homerico foedius, quid Agamemnone in iurgio? nam Aiacem quidem ira ad furorem mortemque perduxit, Tusc.4.52; the example of Ajax extends the point: anger is not only ugly but even fatal. ita sic quoque recte diximus materiam rhetorices esse omnis res ad dicendum ei subiectas . . . Gorgias quidem adeo rhetori de omnibus putavit esse dicendum, ut se in auditoriis interrogari pateretur qua quisque de re vellet, Quint.2.21.21; Gorgias, to be sure, is an example and proof of Quintilian's claim, but the _quidem_ serves to mark a progression beyond the previous thought.

Many of the _quidems_ that are supposed to introduce examples actually perform the familiar task of indicating the first half of a contrast. ipsi illi philosophi etiam in eis libellis quos de contemnenda gloria scribunt nomen suum inscribunt; in eo ipso in quo praedicationem nobilitatemque despiciunt praedicari de se ac se nominari volunt. Decimus quidem Brutus . . . carminibus templorum ac monumentorum aditus exornavit suorum. iam vero ille qui cum Aetolis Ennio comite bellavit Fulvius non dubitavit Martis manubias Musis consecrare, Cic.<u>Arch</u>.27; Brutus and Fulvius, who are paired rather than opposed, certainly cannot be examples of the hypocritical philosopher's own love of glory. est autem inpudens luctus maerore se conficientis, quod imperare non liceat liberis. Dionysius quidem tyrannus Syracusis expulsus Corinthi pueros docebat: usque eo imperio carere non poterat. Tarquinio vero quid impudentius, qui bellum gereret cum is qui eius non tulerant superbiam? <u>Tusc</u>.3.27. haec enim te, nisi ita facies, custos dignitatis (sc. fortitudo) relinquet et deseret. Cretum quidem leges . . . itemque Lycurgi laboribus erudiunt iuventutem . . . Spartae vero pueri ad aram sic verberibus accipiuntur ut multus e visceribus sanguis exeat, <u>Tusc</u>.2.34. vetatque Pythagoras in-iussu imperatoris, id est dei, de praesidio et statione vitae decedere. Solonis quidem sapientis elogium est, quo se negat velle suam mortem dolore amicorum et lamentis vacare. volt, credo, se esse carum suis; sed haud scio an melius Ennius: "nemo me lacrumis decoret, neque funera fletu faxit," Sen.73, "Solon, to be sure, . . . but Ennius . . ." ita fit ut omnino nemo esse possit beatus. Metrodorus quidem perfecte eum beatum putat, cui corpus bene constitutum sit et exploratum ita semper fore. quis autem est iste, cui id exploratum possit esse? Epicurus vero ea dicit, ut mihi quidem risus captare videatur, Tusc.2.17; either autem or vero forms the contrast to quidem (see above, pp. 59-60). (an exordium is sometimes unnecessary) Aristoteles quidem in totum id necessarium apud bonos iudices negat. aliquando tamen uti nec si velimus eo licet, Quint.4.1.72.

Nearly identical with these are the passages in which the quidem is Contrasting quidem solum; the second member is not marked by any adversative word. In the following two passages the members are again linked rather than opposed. "patria est, ubicumque est bene." Socrates quidem cum rogaretur, cuiatem se esse diceret, "mundanum" inquit . . . T. Albucius nonne . . . (still other examples follow), Cic. Tusc.5.108. videsne igitur deorum iudicio, si vident res humanas, discrimen esse sublatum? Diogenes quidem Cynicus dicere solebat Harpalum, qui temporibus illis praedo felix habebatur, contra deos testimonium dicere, quod in illa fortuna tam diu viveret. Dionysius . . . (more examples), N.D. 3.83.

Close to these in turn are the passages where quidem is only Emphatic. No other examples do follow, but quidem vaguely suggests that they could be supplied; we might translate quidem "for one." Since the reference in quidem to something else is not taken up, quidem in these contexts seems to make the person mentioned represent a class; that is to say, it seems to introduce an example. But quidem is really Emphatic. quanti vero ista civitas aestimanda est ex qua boni sapientesque pelluntur? Demaratus quidem, Tarquinii nostri regis pater, tyrannum Cypselum quod ferre non poterat, fugit Tarquinios Corintho, Tusc.5.109, implying that other good, wise men could be named who had done the same. iidemque (sc. Lacedaemonii) de rebus maioribus semper aut Delphis oraclum aut ab Hammone aut a Dodona petebant. Lycurgus quidem, qui Lacedaemoniorum rem publicam temperavit, leges suas auctoritate Apollinis Delphici confirmavit, Div.1.96. tu autem eodem modo omnis causas ages? aut aliquod causarum genus repudiabis? aut in isdem causis perpetuum et eundem spiritum sine ulla commutatione obtinebis? Demosthenes quidem . . . nil Lysiae subtilitate cedit, nil argutiis et acumine Hyperidi, nil lenitate Aeschini et splendore verborum, Orat.110. disputandi ratio et loquendi dialecticorum sit, oratorum autem dicendi et ornandi. Zeno quidem ille, a quo disciplina Stoicorum est, manu demonstra-

re solebat quid inter has artis interesset, Orat.113. de
qua Socrates quidem quid senserit, apparet in eo libro in
quo moritur, Tusc.1.102. Poeni foedifragi, crudelis Hannibal, reliqui iustiores. Pyrrhi quidem de captivis reddendis
illa praeclara: "nec mi aurum posco, etc.," Off.1.38.
quare dabunt mihi aliquam in irascente, deprecante, miseran-
te figuram; scio: sed non ideo irasci, misereri, deprecari
figura erit. Cicero quidem omnia orationis lumina in hunc
locum congerit, Quint.9.1.25.

5. QUIDEM WITH CONJUNCTIONS

Quidem, when used with conjunctions, is most often Emphatic and modifies the clause as a whole; sometimes other uses are found.

Si quidem. (On the scansions sī quidem and sĭquidem, see above, pp. 36-37.) This combination originally meant no more than "if in fact" or "if indeed" and could introduce assumptions of any kind, even contrary-to-fact. In the first two examples an alternative assumption is expressed, so we may call the quidem Contrasting; but, since the alternative is regularly unexpressed and needs to be imagined by the reader, quidem is more often merely Emphatic. siquidem istaec opera, ut praedicas, perfeceris, virtute regi Agathocli antecesseris. sed si non faxis, numquid caussaest ilico quin te in pistrinum condam? Plaut.Ps.531. siquidem hercle possis, nil prius neque fortius. verum si incipies neque pertendes gnaviter . . ., Ter.Eu.50. actumst, siquidem haec vera praedicat, An.465. si quidem vis loqui, non perdocere, ⟨hau⟩ multa longe promicanda oratiost, Naev.com.15. si quidem sis pudicus, hinc facessas, Plaut.Rud.1061. hui dixti pulchre! siquidem quisquam crederet te vivo, Ter.Ph.302. pol si quidem conixus esses, per corium, per viscera perque os elephanti transmineret bracchium, Plaut.Mil.30. Despite this range, however, si quidem naturally tends to appear with the indicative: of the examples cited by Grossmann from Plautus and Terence, fifty are followed by the indicative, seven the present subjunctive, two the imperfect and one the pluperfect subjunctive.

This use of si quidem and the tendency towards the indicative continue in Latin, even after a second use develops. si quidem sit quisquam deus cuii ego sim curae, Turp. com.115. ratiocinati essent etiam atque etiam, quid possent facere, si quidem sua sponte facerent, Rhet.Her.4.16, where we cannot be sure whether the imperfect subjunctive is original or is due to attraction. etiam, si quidem rerum modum figere non possumus, animorum modum tenere possumus, Cic. Parad.25. quid ergo aget Iacchus Eumolpidaeque nostri et augusta illa mysteria, si quidem sacra nocturna tollimus? Leg.2.35. qui latrones igitur, si quidem vos consules? Pis. 24. magnum fecissemus, si quidem potuissemus quo contendimus pervenire, Orat.105. plebes, quodcumque adcidit, pro victis est et in dies magis erit, si quidem maiore cura dominationem illi retinuerint, quam vos repetiveritis libertatem, Sal.Hist.3.48.28. eodem anno Q. Fabius Maximus moritur, exactae aetatis si quidem verum est augurem duos et sexaginta annos fuisse, Liv.30.26.7. non ab exordio usque ad ultimam vocem continuus quidam gemitus et idem tristitiae vultus servabitur, si quidem volet dolorem suum etiam in audientis transfundere? Quint.11.1.54.

Not appreciably different is the use of *si quidem* when it is added as an afterthought, sometimes by a new speaker. We might capture the effect in English by translating "if, that is." Syre, processisti hodie pulchre. -- siquidem porro, Micio, te tuom officium facies, Ter.*Ad*.979. quoniam promissa absolvimus, inquit, eamus. si quidem, inquam, adieceritis de extraordinario pecudum fructu, ut praedictum est, Var.*R*.2.11.1. o pastores nescio quos cupidos litterarum, si quidem nihil istis praeter litteras abstulerunt! Cic.*Flac*.39. 'igitur ne Clodius quidem de insidiis cogitavit, quoniam fuit in Albano mansurus.' si quidem exiturus ad caedem e villa non fuisset, *Mil*.48, heavily ironic, "if indeed he wouldn't have left the villa in order to commit murder." quaero nonne tibi faciendum idem sit nihil dicenti bonum, quod non rectum honestumque sit, reliquarum rerum discrimen omne tollenti? si quidem, inquit, tollerem, sed relinquo, *Fin*.3.13, where again a contrasting force can be felt in the *quidem*. nil moror iussu tuo aperire ferro pectus aerumnis grave. -- si quidem hoc cruenta Tyndaris fieri sinam, Sen.*Ag*.306.

It is easy to understand how *si quidem* passed from this conditional use to a causal one. Used with the indicative *si quidem* can be understood as "if, as in fact is the case." Two similar Plautine passages illustrate this tendency clearly. quem ego hominem, si quidem vivo, vita evolvam sua, Men.903. egone? -- tu istic ipsus, inquam, si quidem hoc vivet (v.l. vivit) caput, Ps.723. In each case the conditional force of si quidem is diminished, and the sense is "as surely as I'm alive." The content of the si quidem clause, once taken to be true, becomes a cause or explanation. "If you are good (as in fact you are), you will be rewarded" becomes "since you are good, you will be rewarded." This development is not completed before the age of Cicero; thereafter si quidem has a double meaning, "since" as well as "if."

In many passages the two can hardly be distinguished since the si quidem clause is patently true; this is often the case naturally when the verb is a past indicative. apud Graecos antiquissimum e doctis genus sit poetarum, siquidem Homerus fuit et Hesiodus ante Romam conditam, Cic.Tusc.1.3. ne ego istas litteras in contione recitari velim, si quidem ille ipse ad eundem scribens in publico proposuit epistulam illam, Att.8.9.2. summa etiam utilitas (sc. inest), siquidem eorum consilio et periculo cum re publica tum etiam nostris rebus perfrui possumus, Mur.24.

In time, though both continue to exist, causal si quidem tends to drive out conditional. Si quidem is exclusively causal in Pliny the Elder, who uses the phrase often, and in Tacitus and Pliny the Younger, who do not; in Quintilian there is but one exception (Ludewig, pp. 50, 52). In the following examples the causal sense is uppermost. similis-que fortuna clarissimorum virorum (sc. Themistoclis et Coriolani), si quidem uterque, cum civis egregius fuisset, populi ingrati pulsus iniuria se ad hostis contulit, Cic.Brut. 42. vide, quaeso, ne tua divina virtus admirationis plus sit habitura quam gloriae, si quidem gloria est inlustris et pervagata magnorum . . . fama meritorum, Mar.26. et philosophi quidem ornate locuti sunt, si quidem et Theophrastus a divinitate loquendi nomen invenit et Aristoteles Isocratem ipsum lacessivit, etc., Orat.62. haec (sc. medicina) nusquam non est, si quidem etiam inperitissimae gentes herbas aliaque promta in auxilium volnerum morborumque noverunt, Cels.proem.1. de cultura agri praecipere principale fuit etiam apud exteros, siquidem et reges fecere, Hiero, Philometor, etc., Plin.Nat.18.22. sed allegoria quae est obscurior "aenigma" dicitur, vitium meo quidem iudicio, si quidem dicere dilucide virtus, Quint.8.6.52. eamque partem Britanniae quae Hiberniam aspicit copiis instruxit, in spem magis quam ob formidinem, si quidem Hibernia medio inter Britanniam atque Hispaniam sita et Gallico quoque mari opportuna valentissimam imperii partem magnis in vicem usibus miscuerit, Tac.Agr.24.1; Ogilvie: "Si quidem . . . provides the justification for a conclusion already stated: 'if, as is assuredly the case, . . .,' 'since.' In G.30,1 and in Cicero it is used, as would be expected, with the indicative. Miscuerit should therefore, be the fut. perf. indic., not the perfect subj." (the latter was the opinion of Kritz, for one). nullius ab eo magistratus ius, nullius auctoritas imminuta est; aucta etiam, siquidem pleraque ad praetores remittebat, Plin.Pan.77.4.

In each of these passages and, so far as I know, in all others where si quidem is causal, the verb is in the indicative, except of course where indirect discourse intervenes. se nihil in vita nisi praeclarissime fecisse, si quidem nihil sit praestabilius viro quam periculis patriam liberare, Cic.Mil.96. illius patientiam paene obsessionem appellabant, siquidem ex castris egredi non liceret, Caes.Gal. 6.36.2, the only si quidem in Caesar; for this reason and also because the si quidem clause only repeats the preceding, Paul, followed by Meusel, removed it from the text. datumque sub iugum tribuniciae potestati consulatum memorantes, si quidem cogi aliquid pro potestate ab tribuno consules et . . . in vincla etiam duci possent, Liv.4.26.10.

Finally some oddities which Ludewig has noted in the usage of Pliny the Elder deserve to be mentioned, for they illustrate the way in which a phrase may become stereotyped, be understood in a new way through analogy, and then start another existence, so to speak. (Si quidem's movement from conditional to causal has already been an instance of this.) Pliny sometimes uses si quidem as if it were a sentence adverb, like nam, and no longer a subordinating conjunction. gignit aliqua et contrarium naturae elementum. siquidem in Cypri aerariis fornacibus et medio igni maioris muscae magnitudinis volat pinnatum quadrupes, Plin.Nat.11.119. Changing the full stop to a comma might, to be sure, remove the anomaly, but the connection is loose and the given punctuation justified. That Pliny has come to understand si quidem as equivalent to quod and therefore to nam, or rather (on account of its position) enim, is a more certain inference from passages like the following, where the phrase does not begin the sentence. magna differentia est et in ipso genere motus, pluribus siquidem modis quatitur, Nat.2.198. idem siquidem oceanus, Nat.2.173. ex homine siquidem, Nat.28.86. (A freakish sentence is: nusquam alibi spectatiore naturae rerum artificio: in magnis siquidem corporibus aut certe maioribus facilis officina sequaci materia fuit, in his tam parvis atque tam nullis quae ratio, quanta vis, quam inextricabilis perfectio! Nat.11.2, where beside other duty the siquidem appears to serve as a Contrasting quidem solum, opposing magnis to parvis.) These most unusual si quidems find one parallel outside Pliny. non ita effusis ac palustribus locis, ut ceterae civitates, in quas Germania patescit: durant siquidem colles, paulatim rarescunt, Tac.Ger. 30.1, "not flat country like the rest of Germany: for the hills go on and on, and only gradually become sparse;" the punctuation of the MSS. (a full stop after durant, siquidem beginning with a majuscule) was corrected by Rhenanus, who is followed by most modern editors. Pliny in one passage has si quidem with accusative and infinitive, a construction also found, though rarely, with _quod_, _quoniam_, _quia_, and _nam_; see Kühner-Stegmann, 2.457. solis fulgore eam (sc. lunam) ut reliqua siderum regi, siquidem in totum mutuata ab eo luce fulgere, Nat.2.45.

Quoniam quidem. _Quoniam quidem_, which first appears in Cicero, is usually no more than a strengthened _quoniam_, "because indeed, in truth." _Quoniam_ alone is sometimes followed by the subjunctive; with _quidem_ it is invariably followed by the indicative. solet haec quae rapuit et furatus est non numquam dicere se emisse, quoniam quidem in Achaiam, Asiam, Pamphyliam sumptu publico et legationis nomine mercator signorum tabularumque pictarum missus est, Cic.Ver.1.60; Asconius detects εἰρωνεία μετὰ συγχωρήσεως. quoniam quidem circumventus, inquit, ab inimicis praeceps agor, incendium meum ruina exstinguam, Sal.Cat.31.9. aut ista bona non sunt quae vocantur aut homo felicior deo est, quoniam quidem quae cara nobis sunt non habet in usu deus, Sen.Ep.74.14. fere autem cum primum partum consummaverunt gallinae, incubare cupiunt ab idibus Ianuariis, quod facere non omnibus permittendum est, quoniam quidem novellae magis edendis quam excudendis ovis utiliores sunt, Colum.8.5.5. sunt aliae causae, magnae et graves, quas a vobis aperiri aequum est, quoniam quidem ego iam meum munus explevi, Tac.Dial.32.7; perhaps _ego_ is emphasized as a contrast to _vobis_.

But the _quidem_ in this combination need not always be

Emphatic. et forsitan in suscipienda causa temere impulsus adulescentia fecerim; quoniam quidem semel suscepi, licet hercules undique omnes minae terrores periculaque impendeant omnia, succurram ac subibo, Cic.S.Rosc.31; as Reisig pointed out,[30] quidem here is Adversative, "perhaps I was rash to take up the case, but because I did take it up, I shall meet and endure all dangers;" Landgraf gives a list of all Ciceronian examples. The quidem of quoniam quidem is Adversative at Dom.69 too, as Nisbet points out.

Quandoquidem. (On the quantity of the o, see above, pp. 36-37.) Quando itself, without quidem, broadened its meaning. Originally temporal ("when"), it became causal ("since") as well, a movement parallel to that of cum in Latin, ἐπεί in Greek. With quidem, however, the word has only a causal meaning. liberem ego te? -- verum, quandoquidem, ere, te servavi, Plaut.Men.1024. dabitur quandoquidem hic volt, Ter.Ad.956. sed sit beneficium, quando quidem maius accipi a latrone nullum potuit, Cic.Phil.2.6. dicite, quandoquidem in molli consedimus herba, Verg.Ecl.3.55. quando quidem, inquit, nostra tueri adversus vim atque iniuriam iusta vi non voltis, vestra certe defendetis, Liv. 7.31.3, and often in Livy at the beginning of a speech, as at 2.12.15, 2.56.9, 6.38.6, et al. nam nisi procedit (sc.

---

[30]Reisig (above, p. 10, n. 9), p. 273.

pastor), stare debet, quandoquidem custodis officium sublimem celsissimamque oculorum veluti speculam desiderat, Colum.7.3.26.

Quandoquidem is regularly accompanied by the indicative. Once Livy uses the subjunctive because the clause is part of indirect discourse, implied. ex suis unum sciscitatum Romam ad patrem mittit quidnam se facere vellet, quando quidem ut omnia unus Gabiis posset ei di dedissent, Liv. 1.54.5. In two other passages indirect discourse is also implied, the reason given being that of the historical figure, not Livy. victus tandem, quando quidem nihil praeter tempus noxae lucrarentur, remissa contione . . . prima luce classico signum profectionis dedit, Liv.2.59.6; also 3.54.2.

Cum quidem. Perhaps by analogy with quoniam quidem and quandoquidem or by association with causal si quidem, the combination cum quidem was developed. Cum is used in all its senses and takes the same mood as it would without quidem; quidem is usually Emphatic.

Cum meaning "when." Catone vivo, qui annos quinque et octoginta natus excessit e vita, cum quidem eo ipso anno contra Ser. Galbam . . . dixisset, Cic.Brut.80, "when indeed." quem magistratum gessi consulibus Tuditano et Cethego, cum quidem ille admodum senex suasor legis Cinciae . . . fuit, Sen.10. quin etiam quaerit (sc. Aeschines) ab ipso (sc. Demosthene), cum quidem eum belvam appellat, utrum illa verba an portenta sint, Orat.26; Sandys reads the indicative and translates "while actually calling, at the moment when;" appellet, the reading of some MSS., is accepted by other editors, who take cum as causal or concessive. Sometimes the cum quidem clause seems an afterthought to the main clause with which it is loosely connected; one might almost understand cum as tum, so independent is it. Tarentum vero qua vigilantia, quo consilio recepit! cum quidem me audiente Salinatori, qui amisso oppido fugerat in arcem, glorianti atque ita dicenti, "mea opera, Q. Fabi, Tarentum recipisti," "certe," inquit ridens, "nam nisi tu amississes, numquam recepissem," Sen.11. idem etiam Socrates, cum apud Delium male pugnatum esset Lachete praetore fugaretque cum ipso Lachete, ut ventum est in trivium, eadem qua ceteri fugere noluit. quibus quaerentibus cur non eadem via pergeret deterreri se a deo dixit; cum quidem ii qui alia via fugerant in hostium equitatum inciderunt, Div.1.123, "when as a matter of fact;" also Div.1.72, Pis.21, Red.Sen.26.

Cum meaning "since." haec cum C. Pontio Samnite . . . locutum Archytam Nearchus Tarentinus . . . se a maioribus natu accepisse dicebat, cum quidem ei sermoni interfuisset Plato Atheniensis, Cic.Sen.41; Reid thinks this temporal, "and indeed at a time when P. was present," but I incline to causal, since the next sentence mentions Plato's visit to Tarentum, presumably to connect Plato with Nearchus' elders. nolo ego Neaeram te vocent, sed Nerienem, cum quidem

Mavorti es in conubium data, Licinius Imbrex com.1.

Cum meaning "although." ibi cum diutius moraretur, P. Scipio Africanus consul . . . voluit eum de provincia depellere et ipse ei succedere, neque hoc per senatum efficere potuit, cum quidem Scipio principatum in civitate obtineret, Nep.Ca.2.2. Like *cum* itself, *cum quidem* occasionally is uncertain in sense. In this passage, for instance, it might mean "although indeed" or "even when:" novissime cum senectute ingravescentem (sc. morbum) viribus animi sustinebat, cum quidem incredibiles cruciatus et indignissima tormenta pateretur, Plin.Ep.1.12.5; some MSS. have *eum* for *cum*. Also Nep.Thr.2.7 and Att. 22.2 ("when" or "although"); see Nipperdey-Witte.

Twice at least *quidem* is clearly not Emphatic and attached to *cum*, but rather Adversative; it introduces the second of two possibilities. quare si quid amice de Romanis cogitabis, non imprudenter feceris, si me celaris; cum quidem bellum parabis, te ipsum frustraberis, si non me in eo principem posueris, Nep.Han.2.6, "when, however" (Rolfe). nam disputandi aut suadendi est aliud idoneum tempus. cum quidem adversarius armatus praesto est, resistendum est huic non verbis, sed armis, Rut.Lup.2.12.

Ut quidem. Unlike the pairs of words above, *ut quidem* is not a genuine combination. *Si, quoniam, quando,* and *cum,* when joined to *quidem,* cohere with it and form distinct idioms. Almost nowhere does <u>quidem</u> belong to <u>ut</u> itself; instead it indicates between one clause and another the same relations as always, Contrasting, Adversative, Extending, etc.

ergo hic ulciscitur, ut quidem sibi videtur; at illa sicut acerbissimam rem maeret, Cic.<u>Tusc</u>.1.105, a Limiting <u>quidem</u> which turns into Contrasting. ut quidem ille dixit mihi qui pueros viderat: ego illos non vidi, ne quis vostrum censeat, Plaut.<u>Men</u>.22, Contrasting <u>quidem solum</u>. nihil non adgressuros homines si magna conatis magna praemia proponantur; ut quidem aliquis tribunus plebis ruat caecus in certamina periculo ingenti, fructu nullo, ex quibus pro certo habeat, patres, adversus quos tenderet, bello inexpiabili se persecuturos, apud plebem, pro qua dimicaverit, nihilo se honoratiorem fore, neque sperandum neque postulandum esse, Liv.4.35.8, "men will attempt anything if great rewards are held out to great daring; <u>but</u> you must neither expect nor demand that a tribune will run great risks with no hope of reward whatsoever;" this, like the two following, is an Adversative <u>quidem</u>. satis praestiterit ratio, si id unum ex dolore, quod et superest et abundat, exciderit! ut quidem nullum omnino esse eum patiatur, nec sperandum ulli nec concupiscendum est, Sen.<u>Dial</u>.11.18.6. reddere est id quod debeas ei cuius est volenti dare. hoc unum mihi praestandum est. ut quidem habeat quod a me accepit iam ulterioris est curae, <u>Ben</u>.7.19.2; also <u>Ep</u>.52.10. suspecta consulis erat mors maxime. necatus a Quarta Hostilia uxore dicebatur. ut quidem filius eius Q. Fulvius Flaccus in locum vitrici consul est declaratus, aliquanto magis infamis mors Pisonis coepit esse, Liv.40.37.6, Extending quidem, "he was said to have been murdered by his wife; when, furthermore, his stepson was made consul in his place, the death of Piso took on a somewhat more suspicious character;" Weissenborn-Müller: "quidem stellt den Satz als Bekräftigung des Vorhergeh. dar." quin etiam deum ipsum tuum ⟨patrem⟩ praecipuam voluptatem operis sui percepisse crediderim. ut quidem isdem vestigiis institisti, quibus parens tuus ingens illud deorum prolaturus arcanum, quae circumstantium gaudia, quam recens clamor, quam similis illi dies, qui hunc diem genuit! Plin.Pan.23.5, Extending also.

ut quidem ego audio, Liv.40.35.13; quidem, which is Limiting, clings to ut, "at least so far as I hear," perhaps not very different from ut equidem audio. In this next passage ut quidem tu may be a dislocated form of ut tu quidem, which is contrasted with the ego following: ut quidem tu quod petisti per pactionem habeas, tot cives incolumes, ego pacem quam hos tibi remittendo pactus sum non habeam, hoc tu, A. Corneli, hoc vos, fetiales, iuris gentibus dicitis? Liv.9.11.9.

Miscellaneous. Several other combinations are found rarely. In each case the quidem is Emphatic.

Nisi quidem, an obvious offshoot of si quidem, but found only in comedy. ita te amabit Iuppiter, ut tu nescis. -- nisi quidem tu mihi quod quaeras dixeris, Plaut.Aul.762. reprehendam ego cuncta hercle una opera, nisi quidem tu haec omnia facis ecfecta, Ps.223.

Ubi quidem, a variant on cum quidem (= "when"). ubi quidem conlega venisset, non passurum quicquam prius agi quam ut . . ., Liv.26.26.7.

Dum quidem, also related to cum. non metuo nec quoiiquam supplico, dum quidem hoc valebit pectus perfidia meum, Plaut.Bac.226, "so long indeed." quae deseri a me, dum quidem spirare potero, nefas iudico, Cic.N.D.3.94. A list of examples is given in Thes. Ling. Lat., 5.2232.

Nam quidem: see examples from Apuleius and Columella, above, p. 18.

Cur quidem: Liv.41.24.7.

At quidem. quid somnias? -- egone? at quidem tu, Plaut.Mos.1014, perhaps equal to at tu quidem, "nay, yourself rather" (Fay); also Mil.659.

INDEX OF PASSAGES

Aetna 458: 24

Am.Mar.14.6.1: 43
   20.4.10: 37
   30.5.7: 53

Apul.Apol.7: 18
   62: 118
   Met.1.1: 24
   2.2: 44
   2.13: 27
   3.7: 28, 33
   3.22: 33
   3.29: 52
   4.8: 33
   7.9: 26
   7.13: 74
   8.10: 27
   9.2: 26
   10.1: 26
   11.26: 52 f.

Auson.Prof.1.5: 24

B. Afr.90.1: 62

Cael.Fam.8.5.1: 28
   8.7.1: 71

Caes.Civ.2.17.2: 79 f.
   2.32.11: 89
   2.32.13: 74
   3.74.2: 71
   Gal.1.40.3: 71
   1.53.6: 102
   3.15.4: 79
   6.36.2: 132
   7.50.4: 92 f.
   7.77.14: 61
   orat.27: 26
   42: 106 f.

Cato hist.95b: 28
   orat.164: 47 f.

Catul.37.15: 116
   64.218: 37
   108.3: 104

Cels.proem.1: 131
   71: 50
   3.3.1: 47
   3.3.3: 33

Chalcidius poet.8: 74

Cic.Acad.1.3: 43
   1.18: 41
   1.25: 113
   1.40: 41
   Amic.8: 49, 62
   9: 97
   12: 55
   13: 70
   26: 40
   33: 99 f.
   79: 84
   Arch.27: 123
   Att.1.1.4: 93
   2.19.1: 111
   4.7.3: 54
   6.1.7: 98
   6.3.3: 87
   7.22.2: 16, 69 f.
   7.23.1: 59
   8.9.2: 130
   10.8.9: 27
   11.6.2: 111
   13.26.2: 25, 42
   13.42.1: 63
   13.45.3: 25
   13.46.1: 49
   14.12.1: 39
   14.12.2: 59, 68

Cic.Att.16.3.4:   101
       16.5.5:   77
       16.9:   14
       16.11.6: 107
Balb.58: 89
Brut.32: 101
     39: 68
     42: 131
     61: 109
     76: 15
     77: 86
     80: 136
    100: 53 f., 108
    110: 40
    143: 108
    227: 39
    229: 115
    231: 37
    259: 76 f.
Caec.8: 83
Catil.2.2: 78 f.
      2.10: 39
      3.11: 48
      3.27: 101
Clu.50: 70 f.
    54: 77
   103: 110
   133: 83
   155: 79
Deiot.22: 67
de Orat.1.70: 86
        2.25: 22
        2.105: 108 f.
        2.289: 113
        3.139: 48
Div.1.72:   137
    1.96:   125
    1.123: 137
    1.128: 47
    2.141: 115
Div.Caec.18: 44
         40: 48
         48: 14
Dom.69: 135
Fam.1.8.1:   79
    1.9.2:   92
    1.9.10: 39
    3.7.5:   46
    6.3.2:   93
    6.6.13: 86
    11.5.2: 27

Cic.Fam.11.14.2: 54
        12.3.1:   73
        12.19.3: 89
        12.25.5: 115
        12.25a.6: 79
        13.16.3: 56
        14.13:   31 f.
        14.4.2:   93
        15.1.4:   41
Fat.46: 105
Fin.1.14:   46
    1.16:   39
    1.26:   108
    1.35:   84
    1.65:   120
    2.23:   98
    2.81:   63
    2.106: 115
    2.118: 5, 6
    3.12:   101
    3.13:   129
    4.13:   29, 108
    4.43:   39, 48 f.
    5.4:   35
    5.6:   43, 63
    5.37:   105
    5.58:   47
Flac.39: 129
Har.30: 33
Inv.1.25: 64
    1.26: 70
    1.36: 46
    1.56: 69
    1.91: 40
Leg.1.52: 97
    2.24: 107
    2.35: 128
    2.69: 112
    3.24: 83
Luc.13: 73 f.
Mar.6:   48
    11: 39
    12: 32, 42
    26: 131
    28: 70
Mil.48: 129
    96: 132
Mur.24: 130
    64: 41
N.D.1.23: 42
    1.57: 15

Cic.N.D.1.79:   83
        1.89:   105
        1.93:   34, 85, 86
        3.15:   74
        3.19:   37
        3.50:   121
        3.78:   49
        3.82:   84
        3.83:   124 f.
        3.94:   141
    Off.1.15:   55
        1.19:   46
        1.33:   105
        1.38:   126
        1.75:   33
        1.95:   39
        2.64:   121
    Opt.Gen.13: 78
    Orat.26:   136 f.
        62:     131
        105:    128
        110:    125
        113:    126
        169:    101
        171:    70
        210:    14
    Parad.25:   128
    Part.122:   113
    Phil.1.20: 57
        2.6:   135
        2.43:   111
        2.51:   99
        2.64:   44
        2.113: 93
        3.16:   93
        3.20:   63
        6.12:   106
        8.12:   70
        10.7:   106
        11.9:   77
        12.23: 97
        14.2:   6
    Pis.10:   77
        21:     137
        24:     128
        25:     89
        78:     45
    Planc.31:   110
        52:     41
        78:     97
        87:     115

Cic.Q.fr.1.1.29:   76
    Quinct.3:   77
        12:     34
        40:     77
        56:     77
    Red.Sen.26: 137
    Rep.1.35:   109
        2.12:   105 f.
        2.21:   22, 39
        3.44:   112
    S.Rosc.31: 135
        41:     99
        138:    28
    Sen.10:   136
        11:     137
        30:     121 f.
        32:     48
        41:     137
        73:     123 f.
        74:     16
        76:     101
        77:     115
    Ses.27:   79
        72:     82
        122:    74
    Sul.54:   101
    Tim.2:   109
    Tusc.1.3:   130
        1.51:   122
        1.98:   92
        1.102: 120 f., 126
        1.105: 139
        2.17:   59, 124
        2.26:   115
        2.30:   105
        2.34:   123
        2.44:   41
        3.12:   112
        3.13:   113
        3.27:   123
        3.48:   83
        4.24:   79
        4.50:   86
        4.52:   16, 122
        4.60:   40
        5.50:   115
        5.108: 124
        5.109: 125
        5.112: 48
        5.115: 96
    Ver.20:   48

Cic.Ver.1.25: 78, 83
    1.60: 134
    2.183: 108
    3.107: 67
    4.3: 93
    4.72: 78
  in Quint.9.3.40: 63

Colum.1.1.10: 18
    1.5.6: 97
    3.9.2: 51
    3.10.18: 116
    4.11.3: 103
    7.3.26: 135 f.
    8.5.5: 134
    8.17.11: 80

Curt.3.1.6: 17
    3.6.10: 34
    4.3.23: 104
    4.7.10: 9
    4.7.25: 102 f.
    4.10.29: 119
    5.5.7: 50
    6.5.3: 67
    6.10.5: 33, 54
    6.10.21: 116
    8.6.1: 72
    8.10.15: 29
    10.1.8: 37
    10.10.6: 90

Enn.scen.166: 99

Fest. p.394 L: 53
    p.462 L: 20

Flor.Epit.1.36 (3.1.11): 52

Fro.Ant.1.p.302 (105N): 104 f.
  Aur.1.p.10 (61N): 52
    1.p.82 (3N): 33
    1.p.194 (79N): 33
  Ver.2.p.294 (116N): 87

Gel.7.16.2: 81
    9.9.4: 52

Hirt.Gal.8.pref.2: 49

Hor.Ep.1.2.13: 87
    1.9.7: 49 f.
    2.1.43: 102
    2.1.69: 54
  S.1.10.51: 107
    2.6.53: 104

Inscr. Dessau 212: 51, 54, 116 f.

Juv.13.19: 51

Licinius Imbrex com.1: 137 f.

Liv.1.14.3: 34
    1.50.3: 43
    1.54.5: 136
    1.57.11: 71 f.
    2.12.15: 135
    2.31.4: 44
    2.56.9: 135
    2.59.6: 136
    3.54.2: 136
    3.68.9: 42
    4.26.10: 132
    4.35.8: 139
    5.33.4: 29
    5.51.4: 25
    6.18.8: 28, 72
    6.34.5: 32
    6.38.6: 135
    7.31.3: 135
    9.3.12: 102
    9.11.9: 140
    10.28.4: 118
    10.40.11: 37
    21.40.8: 50
    21.46.10: 82
    26.26.7: 141
    28.12.12: 109
    28.34.5: 90
    28.34.8: 68
    28.43.7: 114
    30.26.7: 128
    31.29.11: 116
    31.36.3: 70
    32.6.8: 15
    32.32.14: 54
    32.32.15: 15
    32.34.2: 96
    33.38.2: 72

Liv.34.2.3: 100
34.5.3: 116
34.5.8: 111
35.14.4: 45
36.23.1: 33
37.25.12: 113
39.15.4: 104
39.37.20: 50
40.11.7: 110
40.13.2: 110
40.35.13: 140
40.37.6: 139 f.
41.18.11: 67
41.24.7: 141
42.60.2: 69
45.27.11: 56

Luc.3.324: 103
4.472: 81
5.540: 35
8.824: 24
9.685: 72
10.184: 51

Lucil.153: 53
475: 36

Lucr.1.987 (1001): 75
3.904: 33
4.853: 80

Macr.Sat.5.1.13: 47
5.19.21: 53

Mart.1.108.2: 32
10.63.1: 51

Mela 1.2: 72
2.55: 50
2.92: 45

Min.Fel.Oct.14.7: 53

Naev.com.15: 127

Nep.Alc.11.1: 115 f.
Ar.1.2: 109
Att.14.1: 108
22.2: 138
Ca.2.2: 138
Cha.3.4: 32

Nep.Con.2.2: 80
Ep.4.4: 99
Eum.1.1: 39
11.5: 49
Han.2.6: 138
Phoc.3.3: 16
Thr.2.7: 138

Nux 33: 54

Ov.A.A.1.9: 50
Ep.8.75: 54
10.105: 104
Met.3.247: 50
3.557: 80
6.136: 34
10.4: 39
14.338: 45
Pont.2.10.45: 44
Tr.2.139: 34
3.4.1: 50
4.1.66: 45

Paul.Fest. p.248 L: 74

Pers.1.110: 27
5.45: 24

Petr.19.3: 51
40.3: 111
47.13: 17
72.9: 90
99.3: 72
105.5: 28
106.1: 72
117.2: 102
117.8: 91
124.2: 17
127.2: 41
127.6: 28
129.12: 107

Plaut.Am.372: 105
411: 104
610: 89
720: 81
749: 36
855: 100
As.271: 6
645: 111
741: 100

Plaut.As.842:   27 f.
       843:   33, 41
   Aul.762:   141
   Bac.90:   70
       99:    112
       222:   101
       226:   141
       437:   22
       634:   89
       841:   88
       974:   23, 114
       1125: 112
       1177: 88
   Capt.182: 88
        572: 111
        574: 58
        657: 15
        823: 36, 99
        866: 107
   Cas.83:   47
       416:   88
   Cis.515:   78
   Cur.184:   89
   Epid.16:   25
        99:   36
        202: 36
        378: 27
        497: 22
        603: 23
   Men.22:   139
       81:    100
       369:   23
       551:   40 f.
       798:   42
       903:   129 f.
       1024: 135
       1071: 28
   Mer.264:   22
       285:   88
       539:   28
       540:   99
       841:   100
   Mil.30:   127 f.
       259:   112
       368:   112
       520:   37
       547:   53
       650:   22
       659:   141
       988:   99
       1017: 112

Plaut.Mos.178:   104
         208:   98
         235:   99
         909:   29, 114
         944:   107
         1014: 141
         1112: 56
    Per.20:   101
        187:   23
        217:   112
    Poen.295: 112
         588: 78
         601: 114
         1213: 36
         1240: 23
    Ps.223:   141
       531:    127
       620:    22
       723:    130
       1078:   47
    Rud.783:   28
        796:   28
        975:   78
        1061: 127
        1300: 105
        1369: 75
    St.329:   22
       602:    108
       622:    88
       625:    99
       758:    112
    Trin.419: 70
         611: 23
         941: 112
         982: 84
    Truc.667: 100
         808: 99
         832: 109
         963: 101

Plin.Dub.Serm.fr. 95 Della
     Casa: 42
     Nat.2.45: 134
         2.173: 133
         2.198: 133
         2.236: 117
         4.52: 76
         4.91: 76
         5.8:   57
         6.70: 51
         7.27: 97

Plin.Nat.7.158: 117
       7.165:   51
       8.162:   8
       8.178:   117
       9.104:   9
       11.2:   133
       11.119: 132 f.
       12.29:   81
       13.44:   58
       13.120: 46
       15.107: 58
       16.162: 91
       17.90:   81
       17.137: 103
       17.140: 69
       18.22:   131
       18.101: 58
       19.74:   58
       19.189: 76
       21.43:   69
       21.74:   58
       22.36:   58
       25.93:   81
       25.122: 87
       26.8:   99
       28.86:   133
       29.24:   54 f.
       30.116: 117
       32.25:   58
       34.120: 72
       35.10:   29, 108
       36.5:   91
       37.79:   58
       37.169: 57
       37.197: 104

Plin.Ep.1.6.1: 111
       1.12.1: 111
       1.12.5: 138
       2.11.15: 114
       2.14.13: 81
       2.20.11: 52
       3.5.17: 15
       3.6.1:   52
       3.9.12: 73
       3.9.13: 103
       3.15.4: 81
       6.16.13: 110
       7.6.9:   107
       7.7.1:   117
       7.25.6: 117 f.

Plin.Ep.7.27.12: 73
       8.16.1: 118
       10.98.1: 73
Pan.6.3:   37
    23.5:   140
    31.2:   43
    31.6:   52
    59.1:   41
    77.4:   132
    83.2:   13

Priscian Gram.Lat.3.103: 21 f.

Prop.2.3.39: 72
    2.8.28:   50
    2.31.5:   26 f.
    3.12.9:   80
    3.13.3:   107

Prud.Apoth.830: 53
    Peristeph.10.1101: 24

Quint.1.pref.15: 51
    2.5.14:   107
    2.15.8:   117
    2.15.37: 91
    2.21.5:   103
    2.21.21: 122 f.
    3.2.4:   51
    3.11.22: 57
    3.11.26: 97
    4.1.4:   81
    4.1.43:   9
    4.1.72:   124
    5.10.43: 58
    5.12.17: 41
    5.14.33: 33
    6.5.9:   121
    7.1.39:   33, 47
    7.2.53:   73
    8.pref.14: 73
    8.3.17:   81
    8.3.32:   32
    8.6.31:   91
    8.6.52:   131
    8.6.53:   57
    9.1.25:   126
    9.2.57:   46
    9.3.54:   81
    9.3.55:   31
    9.4.52:   110

Quint.10.1.50: 91
    10.1.87: 46
    10.1.88: 51
    10.1.93: 78
    10.1.101: 91 f.
    10.1.107: 62
    10.1.126: 55
    10.2.19: 34
    10.3.1: 47
    10.3.2: 68
    11.1.54: 128 f.
    11.2.23: 29, 104
    12.1.11: 59
    12.1.26: 40
    12.2.15: 78
    12.2.20: 109
    12.4.2: 9
    12.5.5: 42
    12.9.2: 33
    12.9.5-6: 60

Rhet.Her.4.16: 128
    4.37: 70
    4.54: 105
    4.65: 47, 53

Rut.Lup.2.12: 138

Sal.Cat.15.3: 102
    31.9: 134
    51.15: 22
    51.20: 82
    52.11: 27
    58.4: 24
  Hist.1.55.2: 90
    1.77.6: 54
    2.98.4: 104
    3.48.28: 128
  Jug.10.6: 22
    24.9: 28, 41, 49
    85.26: 22
    85.27: 102
  Rep.1.3.2: 22
    2.2.1: 26
    2.6.2: 22
    2.10.4: 22

S.H.A.Eleg.1.6: 68
  Fir.Sat.9.2: 40
  M.Ant.8.8: 59 f.
  Max.12.11: 103

S.H.A.Max.18.4: 111
  Max.Balb.9.1: 69
    14.1: 53
  Op.Macr.1.1: 118
    4.1: 92
  Prob.24.4: 53
  Sev.Alex.32.3: 103
    53.4: 118

Sen.Con.4.pref.2: 72

Sen.Ag.306: 129
  Apoc.4.2: 50
  Ben.2.11.2: 103
    2.18.5: 114
    2.33.3: 72
    3.20.1: 80
    5.3.3: 90
    7.7.3: 50
    7.8.2: 63
    7.19.2: 139
    7.19.9: 9
  Cl.1.5.2: 57
  Dial.1.5.6: 116
    2.13.5: 80
    4.26.4: 77
    5.17.1: 116
    6.4.3: 108
    8.3.1: 72 f.
    10.12.8: 50
    11.18.6: 139
  Ep.11.3: 33
    24.21: 45
    29.4: 33
    33.9: 84
    35.2: 28
    41.5: 50
    52.6: 80
    52.10: 139
    57.6: 46
    71.30: 33
    72.3: 8, 33
    74.14: 134
    74.17: 64
    76.4: 33
    90.45: 103
    99.28: 80
    104.24: 84
    110.1: 46
    115.18: 104
    120.14: 110

Sen.Her.O.1832: 68
    Med.184: 74
    Nat.3.27.10: 111
        6.2.1: 116
    Thy.495: 110

Serv.A.1.576: 21
    Ecl.4.22: 53
    G.1.193: 21

Stat.Ach.1.548: 24, n. 17
        1.806: 44
    Silv.1.2.106: 107
    Theb.3.28: 73
        5.241: 91
        5.735: 103
        7.514: 42
        12.682: 51

Suet.Aug.4.2: 118
        33.3: 33
        64.2: 87
        66.2: 32
        68: 78
    Cl.38.1: 73
    Dom.7.1: 77
    Jul.15: 52
    Otho 1.2: 118
    Tib.41: 35
    Ves.1.1: 40

Tac.Agr.24.1: 131
        33.4: 104
        38.1: 73
        43.3: 117
        44.3: 119
    Ann.1.42: 73
        2.38: 111
        3.12: 55
        3.53: 9
        3.69: 52
        3.73: 32
        4.7: 52
        4.8: 35
        5.5: 52
        5.6: 67
        6.5: 37
        6.48: 117
        6.50: 52
        11.15: 8
        13.12: 117

Tac.Ann.14.55: 14
        15.2: 81
        15.21: 33
        15.71: 52
        16.17: 45
    Dial.3.2: 52
        5.7: 52
        9.3: 43 f.
        32.7: 134
        33.1: 103
        34.5: 111
        35.4: 73
    Germ.6.1: 73
        30.1: 133
    Hist.1.63: 52

Ter.Ad.555: 22
        644: 101
        748: 104
        850: 25
        956: 135
        974: 106, 112
        979: 129
    An.195: 106
        347: 98
        465: 127
        659: 82
        967: 112
    Eu.50: 6, 7, 127
        228: 99
    Hau.547: 104
        606: 101
        632: 22
        775: 113
    Hec.306: 60
        606: 112
        615: 42
        699: 70
    Ph.209: 112
        257: 28, 102
        302: 127
        418: 33
        425: 107
        1003: 47

Traj. in Plin.Ep.10.28: 68
                10.34.1: 52

Turp.com.115: 128

Val.Flac.1.110: 39 f.

Val.Flac.4.476: 111
      6.733: 51
      8.420: 55
      8.432: 74

Var.L.9.32: 104
   R.1.5.1: 26
     1.7.9: 101
    1.22.4: 48
    2.1.13: 114 f.
    2.11.1: 129
    3.12.7: 93

Verg.A.1.238: 74
       1.335: 104
       8.129: 54
      10.105: 37
      10.385: 80
       11.49: 71
      11.348: 104
      11.378: 49
      12.808: 98
     Cat.11.5: 49
     Ecl.1.11: 74
         3.55: 135
          9.7: 104
     G.2.48: 13 f.
      3.217: 102
      4.147: 69
      4.506: 71

Vitr.1.6.4: 116
     2.8.20: 102

www.ingramcontent.com/pod-product-compliance
Ingram Content Group UK Ltd.
Pitfield, Milton Keynes, MK11 3LW, UK
UKHW041418180426
11947UKWH00007B/200